Luther Winther Caws

The unrecognised stranger

and other sermons

Luther Winther Caws

The unrecognised stranger
and other sermons

ISBN/EAN: 9783741160004

Manufactured in Europe, USA, Canada, Australia, Japa

Cover: Foto ©Andreas Hilbeck / pixelio.de

Manufactured and distributed by brebook publishing software (www.brebook.com)

Luther Winther Caws

The unrecognised stranger

THE UNRECOGNISED STRANGER

And other Sermons,

BY THE REV.

LUTHER WINTHER CAWS.

> "O Lord and Saviour of us all,
>   Whate'er our name or sign,
> We own Thy sway, we hear Thy call,
>   And form our lives by Thine.
>
> We faintly hear, we dimly see,
>   In differing phrase we pray;
> But dim or clear, we own in Thee
>   The Life, the Truth, the Way."

LONDON:
H. R. ALLENSON, 30 PATERNOSTER ROW. E.C.
1898.

TO MY DEAR FATHER AND GENTLE MOTHER,
NOW IN HEAVEN,
I DEDICATE THIS BOOK.

Several of these Sermons were preached, and subsequently published in separate pamphlets, some years ago; but they have now been revised and re-written. The verses by H. M. C. were written specially for this volume.

L. W. C.

Biarritz, 1898.

CONTENTS.

I.	THE UNRECOGNISED STRANGER	1— 25
II.	LIVING BY DYING	27— 43
III.	THE LIGHT OF LIFE	45— 63
IV.	UNFINISHED TOWERS	65— 77
V.	THE COMPASSIONATE CHRIST	79—104
VI.	BELLS OF PURE GOLD	106—133
VII.	CHRIST'S THORN-CROWN	135—153
VIII.	THE KINGDOM AND THE KEYS	155—180
IX.	GETHSEMANE	182—201

THE UNRECOGNISED STRANGER.

(S. LUKE 24 C., 13 V.—35 V.)

THE fabled magician, with a drop of ink for his mirror, caused men to see reflected therein the wide, wide world, with its ever-moving panorama of people, events, and things; and in the magic mirror some saw *themselves*.

The truth is we are reflections one of another, and to look into your soul is to catch glimpses of my own.

So S. Luke, with a few strokes of his graphic pen, brings Cleopas and his friend vividly before us, walking and talking there on

THE UNRECOGNISED STRANGER

the road to Emmaus this lovely afternoon. The scene is here; the drama is now passing before our very eyes; the actors are ourselves, and the walk to Emmaus symbolizes our westward way through life. In the magic mirror we see *ourselves*. And herein lies at once the illumination and interest of the memorable tale.

Let us, then, watch these two companions as with eager, thoughtful faces, and sad hearts, they go on their way. Now, they are walking faster, as if to keep pace with their thoughts; now suddenly stopping, as if to clear some important point in the discussion; now, again, walking on in silence. So engrossed are they that all the splendour of the vast Temple of Peace, through which they are walking, appears to attract little or no attention: for, as they talk with one another, thought kindles thought, idea gives birth to idea, question awakens question, reply calls forth reply, Scripture brings Scripture to mind, and while they are musing the fire burns.

THE UNRECOGNISED STRANGER.

Such talks we too have known; epoch-making, character-forming, never-to-be-forgotten talks—the turning points and winding corners of our life-stream—marking and grooving out for us its channel to the great Sea.

Thus it is that to those who put us in possession of our best thoughts and holiest feelings we owe a debt that can never be discharged; for they have opened up springs within us ever fresh and cool through all the hot and weary years. Who gives me a draught of water from the spring strengthens me for one brief hour; but he who brings me some new thought of Christ, quickening my soul with holy love, opens within "a well of water springing up into everlasting life."

Would that our talks with one another were more of the risen Christ, for then He would again draw near and lead the conversation; *and we too might find Him in the next "stranger"*

THE UNRECOGNISED STRANGER.

who shall meet us on life's dusty way!

. . . . . .

What thoughts are those streaming, like dark clouds edged with waves of light, across their minds, as the two companions trudge on over hill and dale, now in the shadows of the already falling day, and now warmed with the slanting sunbeam as it limns their anxious faces with its pencil of gold? What or Who is the theme of theme of their conversation? We live in a world fraught with mystery and robed with beauty; but there is no theme like theirs to touch the deepest chords of the human heart and awake its richest harmonies. What then is it? Is it Science with her marvellous revelations at once humbling and uplifting the noblest intellect? Is it Art with her seductive charms only just unfolding to the artist, whose eye is dim with age, while yet his hunger for the beautiful grows keener every day? Or Music, with nameless subtle witchery thrilling and inspiring

THE UNRECOGNISED STRANGER.

the soul? Or Commerce, with her utilitarian claims too often materializing the spirit in man? Ah no: none of these. Much less are they thinking of those empty nothings over which half our life frivols itself away—a noisy stream babbling over shallows and running to waste!

Listen: for they are talking of *Christ.* Of His sinless life, miracles, kind acts; of His strange majesty and dignity; of His gentleness with the weary, the old, the suffering and sad; of His tenderness towards little children; of His patience with dull, ignorant men; of His wonderful sympathy with penitent wanderers; of His passion to save the wayward and lost. They recall some of those incomparable thoughts which poured like noble music from His guileless lips. They speak of His trial, condemnation, crucifixion, burial in Joseph's tomb, and of His rumoured resurrection and appearance to Mary.

Alas! three days had fled, and the last gleam

THE UNRECOGNISED STRANGER

of hope was just fading from their sky.

They remember His words that He would raise "this temple" in three days. Could He have meant this of his body? Is He really alive again?—or rather have not those passionately devoted women deceived themselves? What if their very love, working upon their over-wrought imagination, has produced the illusion?

For love is mightier than death — KILLS *death — and fills every tomb with white-robed Angels.* The sepulchre wherein we leave our dearest is, like the tomb of Jesus, in a garden, and the garden is sweet with flowers. Thus we bury our loved ones at the gate of life.

And yet, dare they, after all, rely on the fevered imaginations of a few grief-stricken women? If, only, those shrewd, common-sense, unemotional, practical *men*, who went to the sepulchre, had seen Him; "but *Him* they

THE UNRECOGNISED STRANGER.

saw not." Still, did He not himself say that whosoever believes in Him shall never die? And, while Lazarus lay cold in death, did not the Lord say of him "our friend *sleepeth:*" he has not ceased to be, but is simply resting in a more tranquil state. Do we not remember the young man at the city-gate, whose manly limbs, though stretched for the grave, thrilled with warm life again at the Master's touch? Nor can we forget that dear child on whom death lay—

"Like an untimely frost upon the sweetest flower of
    the field:"

Ah! how the small pale face blushed back to life and joy as *His* voice, like far-off music, reached her dull cold ear! If He raised others why should He not himself rise?

And what if once to live, be never to die; but to live again, and for evermore! What if this fleeting life be, after all, merely one short day in the endless succession of glorious days to come? Not a little pool evaporating in the heat

THE UNRECOGNISED STRANGER.

of an hour; but a river flowing from the inexhaustible springs of God! Such were the thoughts and themes stirring and thrilling these two men on the road to Emmaus; and such are the thoughts and themes stirring and thrilling the choicest spirits of the world to-day. For it is the glory of man that, in his sublimest moods, he will listen only to Christ. When once His voice penetrates to the holy of holies within us all, it silences all other voices. "Man shall not live by bread alone, but by . . . GOD."

Yet, like the shadows across their path, as Cleopas and his friend walk on, doubts darken their minds, checkering the bright hopes that anon break through and save them from despair.

Yes; these men are doubters; but not, therefore, sinners. For theirs is not the doubt of would-be unbelievers, but the misgiving of sensitive loving hearts. To confound this kind of doubt with the doubt of cold, unsympathetic, self-willed atheism would be to confound opposites. The latter is mere indifference, or worse; the former the very birth-throes of faith—that true faith which like the rainbow, is born of sunshine and of storm. For there is a fight of faith too often forgotten: nor are the strongest and best—earth's elect ones—those who have never known doubt, but those who have struggled with the mysterious visitor all through the long night, and have found themselves new men in the morning; men with the marks and with the blessing of the struggle upon them, *because they have learnt therein the limits of their strength.* Israel feeling his weakness and halting as he walks, is a much nobler man than Jacob ignorant, self-confident, and bold. And it is only through the struggle that we become princes; it is only when we have learnt our weakness and ignorance, that a new name is given us, and we too are able to prevail with God and with men.

For there is a right kind of Rationalism.

THE UNRECOGNISED STRANGER.

There is a devout, reverential spirit, feeling mystery everywhere, yet conscious the while that the Great Darkness is only the blindness of eyes too weak to bear the blaze of excessive LIGHT. This is not the Rationalism, which, because it cannot evacuate life of mystery, charges confusion upon God: it is the spirit which feels that the mystery lies in our own limitations.

Our darkness is God's light; and *those very doubts, so often troubling and darkening sensitive souls, are but the shadow of Jesus as He is drawing near.*

 . . . . . .

" And it came to pass that while they communed together, and *reasoned*, Jesus himself drew near and went with them."

Thus these two disciples are Rationalists, but of the right sort; for there is a kind of

THE UNRECOGNISED STRANGER.

reasoning which brings Jesus near. Yes, it is so; and when we touch the deepest in ourselves we are nearest to *Him*. It is when we reveal to each other our tenderest yearnings and our most sacred hopes and fears, that the mysterious "Stranger" draws near, and adds Himself to our number. It is when our talk takes on the nobler tone that the music of Heaven steals into it. It is often by telling our doubts to a friend that they are solved: for he may speak just the illuminating, guiding word; or, if he cannot, it may console us to know that one so much better and cleverer than ourselves is living out his Christly life content to wait for the solution of some problems "till the day break and the shadows flee away."

Now, the conversation of Cleopas and his friend is *overheard;* but so ennobling and inspiring it is that had they known Who was near they could not have wished it otherwise. There was grandeur, if great severity, in the

THE UNRECOGNISED STRANGER.

Puritan idea of our life being ever under

"The great Task-master's eye."

This conception reveals the Puritan's view of what Carlyle would call "the Eternal Verities;" but it is touched with austerity far more likely to terrify than to persuade.

S. Paul knew the human heart better when he wrote,—"knowing, therefore, the terror of the Lord, we *persuade* men": and if Christ-lovers would bear in mind Who is always listening to them, their very loyalty to Him would raise their talk to a higher key and richer tone.

But the "Stranger" has joined them, and at once the central figure of the three, He attracts and absorbs our attention. A nameless something in that figure rivets eye and ear, and we almost forget the man on either side.

S. Mark says "He appeared unto them in ANOTHER FORM." (S. Mark 16 c. 12 v.)

THE UNRECOGNISED STRANGER.

Perhaps the baptism of suffering of those three days had scarred and changed his features? But what signifies the "form"? Omnipotence can clothe itself in any form, from the lightnings and thunders of Sinai to the sweet babe in the manger of Bethlehem. *We never know in what "form" Christ may be drawing near!* O for the eye to see, the ear to hear, the heart to feel. Give us these and Christ will shine in every star, look through every flower, illumine every horizon, speak in every harmony that thrills the soul; and we shall feel *Him* in every touch of dear human love that warms and cheers the world.

Now, Jesus did not come to them in the old, familiar form; therefore they saw in him only "a Stranger."

Yet listen. He comes to men in myriad forms. Ten thousand are the avenues to the soul, and the Christ of yesterday has changed His form to-day. The Christ of unthinking boy-

THE UNRECOGNISED STRANGER.

hood is not the Christ of mature manhood; for since those early days both He and we have suffered, and this suffering has changed both His form and ours. Ever the same in heart and purpose, yet He is ever assuming fresh forms and methods as the years roll on. There is a sense in which Christ is *transfigured* every day.

When shall we learn and understand that Christ is always appearing to his people IN ANOTHER FORM? Cleopas and his friend failed to recognise Him because they knew Him only in the old form. Unconsciously they prejudged the case; and what is so blind as *prejudice?* To look for Christ only in such forms as we have known Him is to walk the world with eyes holden, and to see merely "a stranger" where Christ himself is. This is why the Church of yesterday cried "heresy," where to-day she gladly and thankfully recognises Christ! But there is such a thing as "crucifying Him afresh"; there is an awful blindness seeing no Christ where

THE UNRECOGNISED STRANGER

only Christ is!

Who remembers that He is still the helpless babe, the child in the temple, the dutiful youth at home, the young mechanic at his bench, the worn-out voyager asleep in the storm, the healer by our beds of pain, the teacher in our streets, the solacer by our graves, the happy guest at our feasts of joy, the quiet visitor thankful for our hospitality, the tired man begging a draught of water from our well, the poor outcast who has not where to lay his head, the stranger walking by our side, the man transfigured with the shining light of Heaven, the suppliant in agony and bloody sweat, the forsaken and betrayed friend, the suffering and dying man?

Who understands that *the story of the unrecognised Stranger is the oft-repeated tale of history—our own personal, daily history?*

THE UNRECOGNISED STRANGER.

How often have even apostles and disciples wished to call down the fire of heaven upon those who do not talk Religion with their own peculiar accent; and who cannot pronounce, without the taint of suspicion, their doctrinal pass-words and theological shibboleths!

Meanwhile, who bears in mind that the Holy One cannot be limited in His operations, and that the revelations of Christ to the soul are as manifold as the ever-varying, innumerable needs of our frail humanity?

Yet, how sorrowfully slow we are in learning the very obvious lesson that Christ is none the less Christ because appearing in some strange or unconventional form.

Now He assumes the form of George Fox's swift inspirations, or of John Wesley's ordered methods and apostolic zeal; and now He walks and talks with us in the exquisite sermons of

THE UNRECOGNISED STRANGER.

Robertson or Newman. Now He is throbbing in the brain and heart of William Carey as the restless little man dreams the dream of all the world for Christ; and now He is suffering the lingering death of leprosy in the body of "Father" Damien. Now He is stirring our pulses through the seraphic spirit of C. H. Spurgeon; and now He appears in another form and enlightens our understanding by the fresh, original thinking and the pure, saintly life of Henry Drummond. Or yet again He is drawing near in some forward step of Science which tends to lessen misery and assuage pain and grief.

FOR EVERYTHING WHICH MAKES FOR THE WELL-BEING OF MANKIND IS CHRIST'S.

"He that is not against us is for us."

But the word of the Master is more personal still. Alas for these dull, purblind eyes

THE UNRECOGNISED STRANGER

of ours: alas that we too are so slow of heart to understand that it is He, and none other, Who is walking and talking with us on our westward way; alas that, with us also, the day is far spent and the shadows are deepening around before our sight is cleared, and we are able to see, to recognise, and to rejoice in the Beatific Vision.

Till that hour of illumination we see men "as trees walking," and call things by wrong names. Jesus is often near us in our loneliness and grief, but like Mary, we mistake Him for the gardener.

In the train, yesterday, we met "a stranger," —only a stranger,—yet Christ was there! We saw only "a starving child," where Christ lay perishing for lack of bread and love. Or that boy with soulful face and lustrous eyes, so hungry for knowledge yet teaching us so much, to whom life is already so august and sacred—

THE UNRECOGNISED STRANGER.

"my Father's business"—we thought he was merely the son of Joseph and Mary; while in the tired man who begged a draught of water from our well we saw only "a Jew" and did not dream that he was anything more!

One day the scales will fall,—"And the King shall answer and say unto them, Verily I say unto you, Inasmuch as ye have done it unto one of the least of these my brethren, ye have done it unto ME."

O strange ophthalmia that held our eyes!

We often find ourselves praying for "more light":—but what we really need is MORE LOVE.

Do you remember a dear wrinkled face lined with sacred sorrow? It was your Mother's face. Gentle, patient mother; always living Christ, and sometimes taking you aside and talking of

THE UNRECOGNISED STRANGER.

Him. But you were a child, seeing and hearing only your mother; for your eyes were holden, nor did you then realize that *Christ* was bending over you in her frail form.

.   .   .   .   .   .

And now the two are silent as the stranger "expounds unto them in all the Scriptures the things concerning himself." A magic spell is upon them, thawing their hearts but freezing their lips! His words are so entrancing they cannot speak but only listen. Wondrous Companion! As He talks, old things are passing away and all things are becoming new. A new Bible is in their hands; the prophets are speaking to them now with new voices; new light—light which, somehow, sheds a halo round the Stranger beside them — is flooding their minds; "DEEP CALLETH UNTO DEEP."

Meanwhile, the day is dying, and the long shadows of the hills are creeping across the

THE UNRECOGNISED STRANGER.

valleys, like dark headlands in a sea of gold. Far behind, the city of Jerusalem flashes back the sunset, as the sun himself is just sinking into the tomb of Night. But a few short hours and the sun and city shall greet each other in the fresh, new dawn. On such an evening who can be deaf to the anthem of praise and hope ringing to the vault of Nature's glorious Temple? "This is none other but the House of God, and this is the gate of heaven."

But now the end of the journey is near, and the stranger makes as though he would go further. The music ceases; the dream is vanishing away. Now, at length, they feel how grand and how precious is the stranger's gracious companionship; they beg Him, with hearts aglow, to be no longer stranger, but friend— "and they constrained Him, saying abide with us."

Not till He is going from them do they fully realize His worth.

THE UNRECOGNISED STRANGER.

So slip from us the most sacred opportunities of life before we begin to understand their priceless value. Youth, with its innocence and open-eyed wonder, comes, like sweet spring, white with the blossoms of thick-thronging hopes and fancies, and has glided by before we awake to its rare worth and beauty. In our dulness of comprehension, nay more in our waywardness, we rebelled against the protectings and guidings of tender love as though they were but irksome restraints. We understand, now, that all those moulding influences about us from our cradles until this hour;—THE DIVINE ENVIRONMENT OF LIFE—*are only the garb of the so-long unrecognized Christ who has lovingly walked by our side the long journey through.* "I girded thee though thou hast not known me."

Or some human friendship once was ours; so helpful, pure, noble—but we took it as a mere matter of course, lightly esteeming its loving sympathy, wise counsels, frank rebukes, generous

THE UNRECOGNISED STRANGER.

praise, and its long-suffering patience. But when our journey together neared its close, and we realized that our friend was going from us, leaving us alone in the gathering darkness—then we felt, as never before, how precious the love now slipping away, and our heart cried in sorrow and pain—"Abide with us."

. . . . . .

"And it came to pass as He sat at meat with them, He took bread, and blessed it, and brake, and gave to them." (S. Luke 24 c. 30 v.)

Once more the conversation deepens and heightens, and His voice is heard in thanksgiving and prayer. Its tones are unmistakeable now; at last their dull ears, and dim eyes are opened, they recognize Him, "And He vanished out of their sight:" or, as the margin reads "He ceased to be seen of them."

For, perhaps, some hours, they had been

THE UNRECOGNISED STRANGER.

seeing and hearing only "a stranger;" but now, for one brief instant, the film and mists part and they see CHRIST.

All that was strange and unfamiliar has fallen away, and, beyond all doubt, they know Him now. The Soul is, at length, awake, and the vision is hers. The inward revelation is made—the outward apparition gone. Now that the spiritual vision is theirs, what need of the bodily presence? Now that they *"know,"* what need for further seeing? For one instant, only, they see Him. It is enough. *The visions of the Soul are eternal.* Once to see Christ is to see Him for evermore.

The Rainbow fades from the eye, but not from the soul. It is only the "form" that disappears; the Vision abides.

It is the "stranger" who vanishes — but CHRIST remains: "Lo I am with you alway."

THE UNRECOGNISED STRANGER.

And now, with beating hearts, they recall to one another the wonderful talk of the "Stranger" whose flashes of thought, penetrating their dark minds, had revealed the Scriptures to their understanding, their own hearts to themselves, and, in the stranger by their side, CHRIST, who was dead but is alive for evermore.

It was their own dulness and slowness—their *soul-drowziness*—which had held their eyes and turned Christ into a stranger. But, now, as their minds run back to the journey just over, they feel again the burning within, and know that only He could thus have set their souls on fire.

Look back : and, as your eye follows the road stretching far behind across the fields of memory, you too will recognize Another with you all the journey through, and with you still ; and His Form is like unto the SON OF GOD.

LIVING BY DYING.

"Whosoever shall seek to save his life shall lose it, and whosoever shall lose his life shall preserve it."—S. LUKE 17 C., 33 V.

O F all the utterances of Jesus this is one of the sublimest and most profound.

A striking paradox it is nevertheless a simple, solemn truth, whose roots reach down into the deepest places of human life and thought: it is the declaration of that mighty law upon which, as upon eternal rock, rests the glorious superstructure of all life, whether of man, beast, or tree. For there is no finding except by losing, no getting but by giving, no living save through dying.

LIVING BY DYING.

Nature's cradles are graves, and her graves are cradles. The rotting leaves of Autumn, strewing forest, lane, and field, reappear in the sweet spring flowers, and everywhere death is "the gate of life." The assertion of S. Paul—"I die daily," is as applicable to physical as to spiritual life, and finds its verification in the infant's cry, the lion's roar, and the lily's decay. From inception to cessation, life is a constant double process of waste and renewal, for is not every breath a loss of vital force as well as the means of its sustentation? Nature gives with one hand while she takes away with the other, and this perpetual balance is what we call life.

Now, grasping this obvious law, and bearing in mind its equal application to physical and spiritual life, we hold the key to the golden secret of our text, while the truth it contains is borne in upon the mind from every corner of Creation—a glorious light, whose splendour streams in

LIVING BY DYING.

through a thousand windows upon the devout and reflective soul.

True, indeed, the words themselves are simple, homely, common-place: one might read them many times without catching flashes from the battlements of Heaven, or lurid gleams from the gates of hell—yet life and death are both here, the rosy sunlit peaks far above the clouds, and the black abysses and awful gorges beneath them when once the eye looks through the mists.

For what is meant by "*saving*" life but the right use of its noblest powers, and what is meant by "*losing*" it but the wrong use, and, therefore, the prostitution and final loss of those powers?

The subject now branches before us into two main lines of thought—viz.:
The Pathway of Death.
The Pathway of Life.

LIVING BY DYING.

The Pathway of Death.

According to the text this is *selfishness;* making self the chief end and aim of life; living as if life were a dowry to be selfishly squandered, and not a stewardship to be faithfully discharged. Now, it is admitted that every man possesses the instinct of self-preservation, and no man can discharge his obligations to mankind who is not also loyal to himself.

> "To thine own self be true,
>   And it must follow as the night the day
>   Thou canst not then
>   Be false to any man."

But while self-preservation is right and obligatory upon all, self-seeking as the rule of life is a wicked, woful and disastrous mistake. Self-care for the sake of others is good and right; but to love self *to the neglect of others* is both sinful and suicidal, for selfishness, "when it is finished, bringeth forth death."

Christ did not seek to save self; on the contrary, He continually *gave* self—" for their sakes I sanctify, [*i.e.*, devote] myself;" and again, "Even Christ pleased not himself;" "Who though He was rich, for your sakes became poor"—"who gave himself a ransom for all," and of His life Jesus said—" No man taketh it from Me, but I lay it down of myself." Self-giving, therefore, was the law of Christ's life.

Now, think of physical strength. The blacksmith at his flaming forge cannot "preserve" his strength by folding the arms and avoiding exertion; for folded arms mean flaccid muscles, and the sure leaking away of muscular power. No—there is only one way of preserving his strength, viz., by beating it away day by day upon his sounding anvil. *He gives to get, and loses to find.* Again, one of the simplest conditions of health is exercise—but exercise involves expenditure of vital force, the giving away of physical energy; for the law of natural life is waste that you may grow, die that you may live;

in a word, lose self to find self. And Nature, who is a kind mother to the obedient, is an implacable judge when disregarded or defied; and sooner or later she invariably breaks every offender across her mighty wheel!

This is the hell whose scorching flames leap from the text, that terrible hell of *Retribution* which always treads upon the heels of transgression, the hell King Solomon saw when he wrote " whoso breaketh an hedge a serpent shall bite him."

True, there is in Nature just a narrow fringe of mercy with which, as if loth to punish, she for a little while graciously covers the transgressor, but once beyond that narrow fringe, and destruction is sure and often terribly swift. For proof of this look around.

Ask the sensualist, whose base passions have consumed him as with fire, leaving his body a

LIVING BY DYING.

mass of living corruption, and rendering life, once a sweet blessing, now an intolerable burden, whether in the endeavour to find life he has not lost it, whether in the search for happiness he has not found most abject misery?

Ask the satiated worldling if, in making self-gratification his life-long aim, he has not lost the keen sensibility to pleasure he once possessed, so that the delights of earlier years now cloy upon the taste? Like the thumbed-out strings of a harp, he is unresponsive to the old touch—the music is gone. Let the poor drunkard say whether while seeking to gratify appetite he has not wrecked character, ruined health, and destroyed happiness?

The solemn truth is, that having all taken self-gratification as the rule of life they have all reached the same sad end — self-destruction: seeking to save themselves they have lost themselves.

LIVING BY DYING.

And just as exercise is essential to full vitality and perfect health, so activity is the law of spiritual life and growth. Those higher faculties—Faith, Hope, Love, which are the distinguishing glory of man and his flower and crown, must be kept active or they will die.

"We grow good by DOING good;" and *the sinews of the soul, no less than the muscles of the body, shrink and waste away unless they are kept in full play.*

Fold the arms and lose your strength : bury your talent and suffer the awful penalty of its final and irretrievable loss. Of every talent it is true—use or lose. Defy or disregard this law —the law of spiritual activity—and you are sliding down the pathway which ends in death : but obey it, bend to it and your chariot is linked to the stars, for God is with you. Or, changing the figure, your sails are arched to the breeze blowing fair for the celestial Haven.

LIVING BY DYING.

There is a legend that a renowned warrior, wrapping himself in a poisoned mantle put in his way by the enemy, lay down and slept. Awaking, he found, when too late, that he was a doomed and dying man. That poisoned mantle is *self*.

And even so every man who wraps himself round with slothful selfishness, who buries himself in himself, and keeps himself to himself shall certainly destroy himself—for this is the verdict of reason no less than the solemn assertion of reason's Lord—" Whosoever shall seek to save his life shall lose it."

Turn we now to consider secondly :
The Pathway of Life.
This, Jesus declares to be self-denial, perfect self-surrender, the human will lost in the Divine : for " whosoever will lose his life for My sake shall find it."

That is a thrice-hallowed moment when the

LIVING BY DYING.

soul first awakes to the real meaning of existence, and the vision of God, breaking like sunlight through morning mists, floods the heart with strange, new joy. Henceforward a new ideal dominates the mind; Christ's conception of life becomes ours, while old thoughts and feelings fall from us as worn-out Autumn leaves fall off and make place for the new buds beneath. We realize "the expelling power of a new affection." Our former selfishness, reserve, indifference and coldness, begin to break up and float away like icebergs at the touch of Spring. For now we see men with Christ's eyes, we listen to their sad, confused cries of sin, suffering, and death with His ears, we feel their sorrow and joy with His heart, we are baptized with His baptism and begin to enter into "the fellowship of His sufferings," our soul like His is "troubled," our crown like His becomes a crown of thorns, and our burden like His is sometimes more than we can bear—the sweet pain of the Redeemer's cross has touched us, and "we know that we have passed from death

LIVING BY DYING.

unto life because we LOVE." For now we see in our brother one for whom the Son of God gave himself, the Cross is the measure of man's greatness and worth, and the sublime passion fills us to seek and save the lost.

This, this is Life—self-devotion to man for Christ's sake, self-surrender to His will, self lost in God and found again in love to man, *for he only has Life in whom the life of Christ is being lived over again*—"I live, yet not I, Christ liveth in me."

Take, as a striking illustration, that noble lady whose fine heroism has shed a new glory and sacredness upon womanhood, Florence Nightingale. What is the secret of her immortality? Self-sacrifice. That holy, Christ-begotten passion called "the love of Christ," constrained her, and forgetting self, sinking self, losing self, she found her true self in that thrice blessed work. And in many an unknown life it

LIVING BY DYING.

is quiet submission in suffering, patient endurance of wrong, brave continuance in well-doing, and a sweet serenity and elevation of character which are the sign-manual of the Redeemer and the seal of LIFE upon the foreheads of the Redeemed.

That such self-denying, Christly lives involve suffering, one need not add, for who can bear the world's sin and not be bowed beneath the burden? Who can love men as Christ did and not himself be "a man of sorrows and acquainted with grief?" Who can look upon the dark social problems in England to-day, notably in our wickedly-overcrowded cities and not weep with Jesus over the city?—nay, who can possess His spirit and not do as He did, shed not tears only but blood and life!

For oh, the poverty, wretchedness, filth, ignorance and crime surging around our doors are almost enough to paralyze hope and break the heart for very pity and shame.

LIVING BY DYING.

At the gilded gate of our boasted, modern civilization many a Lazarus lies "full of sores" while Dives feasts and dances within.

The unconcern of the rich, no less than the misery of the poor, is a leprous spot upon our social system.

Here and there are a few Christ-inspired men and women spending themselves in a well-nigh hopeless endeavour to stem the torrent of wretchedness and death; but what do the vast majority of professing Christians care for the multitudinous lost?

Give us comfortable homes, beautiful houses of prayer, with musical choirs, smoothly-cushioned pews, smoothly-talking preachers, and the gates of Heaven are open before us!

Ah, me!—where is the quick sympathy, the tender compassion, the intense love, the grand self-devotion, the splendid enthusiasm of the Nazarene Carpenter?

Let none decry beautiful and inviting places of worship, or underrate the ministry of music and of eloquence; but these are not all.

O, sirs, shall the Church of Christ be rocked in an everlasting lullaby while the blood of the wounded and weary by the world's highway cries like the blood of murdered Abel from the ground? Can the answer of guilt clear our conscience— "Am I my brother's keeper?"

While we spend ourselves in selfish indulgence, or in theological hair-splittings and quibblings about doctrine, men are perishing for lack of love, for, say what we will, *it is not doctrine the world is dying for, but real Christ-love.*

The serious problems before the Church to-day are not speculative but practical—the

LIVING BY DYING.

starving, the naked, the ignorant, the lost—will you feed, clothe, teach and save these?

This is the point which decides between the up-grade and the down. Failing here we are on " the down grade " whatever our creed.

As for religious beliefs, so long as men think they will differ, and let every man love his brother and not speak bitterly against him.

Let men and women study the Scriptures for themselves, and having formed an intelligent creed mould their life upon it; but *let every doctrine perish that leaves the heart cold and loveless.*

Christ-love is the one thing—INDISPENSABLE.

The Priest and the Levite were the custodians of the noblest creed known to the world before

LIVING BY DYING.

Jesus came, the creed of Abraham, Moses, David, Daniel and Isaiah, but they broke down completely over the wounded man!

The good Samaritan's creed was to "pour in oil and wine;" his own hand dressed the wounds, his own beast carried the sufferer, his own money supplied his wants. And it is along this path—the path of self-sacrifice, the path of real love, that the footprints of the Redeemer are found, and where also lies the shadow of the Cross cast there by the Heavenly radiance that streams from behind it. No cross, no crown, *sic itur ad astra*—such is the way to the stars.

" If we suffer we shall also reign with Him." And what is it to suffer with Christ? It is to feel the sin and suffering of men as though our own, because our brothers'; it is to be in heart-touch with the sin-stained and lost; it is to be thrilled with the world's pains, groans and tears, and to spend ourselves in alleviating its sorrow; it is to

LIVING BY DYING.

live and die for men as Christ himself also did. This, this is the pathway of Life. And for all who thus continue with Him in His temptations, a kingdom is appointed ; they shall in that day be with Him where He is, and beholding His glory and sharing in the Redeemer's final triumph over sin, sorrow and death, they shall be for ever filled with His joy, and shall sit down with Christ upon His Throne.

THE LIGHT OF LIFE.

"In Him was life; and the life was the light of men." S. JOHN 1 C., 4 V.

"He that followeth Me shall not walk in darkness, but shall have the light of life."
S. JOHN 8 C., 12 V.

IT is said that the poet Tennyson while once walking in his garden with a friend, was asked what he thought of Christ? Stopping over a little flower, the poet answered—"What the Sun is to this flower Christ is to my soul."

And what *is* the Sun to the flower? It is its light, its life, its loveliness—in a word its all in all: for were there no Sun, there could be no flower. Every flower grows in the Sun; and

THE LIGHT OF LIFE.

without light there could be no life. Could we extinguish the Sun what would become of this tiny planet? Where would be the fresh, sweet Spring, blossoming in beauty; where the foliage and flowers of Summer; where the rich, ripe fruits of Autumn?

But as without light, no life; so, without light there could be no beauty, no delightful harmonies of colour, no green landscapes with their infinite gradations of shade and hue; no blue sky bending over all. For light holds within its mysterious power not only the gift of life, but also the secret of all loveliness. It is not simply the great life-giver; it is, too, the bestower of all beauty; since all colour resides in the light, which softly clothes the world with its own loveliness. *Light is the soul of life, and of beauty.*

Is it not then most striking that Christ, by whom as S. John tells us, all things were made, should single out this supremely precious

THE LIGHT OF LIFE.

and indispensable boon as the natural counterpart and physical emblem of Himself? For Christ plainly means that He is to our *soul* all that light is to our natural life.

Pursuing this line of thought the theme unfolds before us as
> *Christ our Light,*
> *Christ our Life, and*
> *Christ our Loveliness.*

CHRIST OUR LIGHT.

We have no greater need than light: for life is thick-palled with darkness—dense darkness that can be *felt*. Who can unriddle life's awful but sublime mystery? Who can open the sealed book and tell us the secret of God? Who can bring out the harmony that runs through all the seeming discords of our frail humanity, with its rhapsody of bliss and hope, its long-drawn agony of sin, anguish, doubt, and despair? The Agnostic cannot help us; for we know his honest but sorrowful confession that he cannot discover a Divine Father on the throne of the Universe, but only "inscrutable power." And so the human intellect roves like a flash-light through the night, feeling thick darkness everywhere. But there is a pillar of fire guiding us through the dark waters, and shedding its ruddy glow across the trackless sands of the desert. This mighty, guiding beacon, is Christ Himself, to all who trust and follow Him "the light of life," but to those who neither believe nor obey, "a pillar of cloud and darkness."

To Him, therefore, we turn and say, with S. Peter, "Lord to whom shall we go? *Thou* hast the words of Eternal life." For Christ, who takes no limited view, as we do from our little standpoint in Time, but whose glance comprehends Eternity, and who sees the final issues of all things clear before Him—tells us to have faith in God, for the Supreme Power is LOVE!

THE LIGHT OF LIFE.

This is the LIGHT that strikes its pathway of gold through the ages, and leads us on and up to our Father in Heaven.

Now, in Christ was life, and that life was "the light of men." Would we know the meaning, the purpose, the joy, and the grandeur of life—then let us live as He did: let us receive Christ into our soul as the flower drinks in the Sun.

And what a marvellous *revealer* light is. Have you seen the dawn on the mountains? those far-flashing peaks of flame?—below us, valleys, rivers, winding roads, villages, forests, meadows, grazing cattle—all there, flooded with sweet light. All things now appear in their true relation, each to each, because the Sun has risen driving darkness and ignorance away. So Christ, when He came, dispelled the darkness of the world. Before Christ came even the elect spirits of mankind held but poor and imperfect conceptions of the Divine Being. Even Moses saw

THE LIGHT OF LIFE.

Him at a distance, 'midst the thunders and lightnings of Sinai, and trembled at the sublime Vision. Even Elijah caught only glimpses of His passing Form, and wrapt his face in his mantle for very fear.

Hence, speaking generally, the God of the Old Testament is the Almighty Creator, a glorious Monarch, fearful in praises and doing wonders: but the God of the New Testament is the Divine Father whose heart throbs with yearning love and who waits to forgive. All this we learn from Christ in whom the heart of God is revealed: for is not Christ the " Word "—that is to say the *spoken thought* of God? " He that hath seen Me, hath seen the Father."

All that our finite minds can know of the incomprehensible One we may know through Jesus Christ. And were it given to us to climb higher and know more—even then there would still be an horizon, a boundary line beyond which

THE LIGHT OF LIFE.

we could not see. For only the Infinite Himself has no horizon and sees all things as they are.

Now, we know that the scientist cannot take the mighty Sun himself into his little laboratory, but he can learn a great deal about the glorious Orb of day by analyzing a single ray of light. From as much of the Sun as he can see, and so to say handle, he may get to know secrets hidden from the common eye. So we may know God as it has pleased Him to reveal Himself in Christ Jesus: for "this is life eternal that they may know Thee and Jesus Christ whom Thou hast sent."

.   .   .   .   .   .

But Christ not only reveals God to men; He discovers men to themselves: *for in the light that shines from Christ men stand self-revealed* —just as we feel most our own shortcomings when in the presence of some superior spirit.

THE LIGHT OF LIFE.

It was when S. Peter came near to Christ that he cried,—"I am a sinful man, Oh Lord." For the beauty of holiness that shone from Christ flooded the dark mind of the impulsive and wayward man with a light in which he saw himself; as the morning sunbeam shows the prisoner the foulness of his cell. Nor can we ever know ourselves until we know Christ; for when He opens our blind eyes we first see Him and then ourselves. Simple and beautiful but very deep withal was the prayer of the peasant boy,— "Lord, shew me Thyself, that I may see myself."

Further, *Christ reveals Heaven and the future life in strong, clear light.* Of that grander, fuller life beyond the grave He always speaks without the faintest shadow of a doubt: with the assurance and authority of One who has come from that Land and whose home it is. "In my Father's house are many mansions." Heaven is no supposititious or imaginary dream-land away over broad, unknown seas; it is not even a

THE LIGHT OF LIFE.

mysterious bourne whence there is no return—it is simply "My Father's house." It is peace, bliss, rest—"to day thou shalt be with Me in Paradise."

Between that glorious life and this hangs the misty veil that men call *death;* but when we have passed through the mist, there stretching before us in vernal beauty, our eyes shall see the sunlit hills and plains of Heaven.

I remember one day on the north-east shores of the Isle of Wight. All day long the fog had clung in white folds to the sea, obscuring everything. But, towards sundown, suddenly the fog-curtains rolled up, and the evening light, breaking along the shore across the Solent, flamed upon a thousand windows in the city over there. Someone said "how beautiful;" and a voice within me seemed to be saying—" In My Father's house are many mansions; if it were not so I would have told you."

. . . . . .

THE LIGHT OF LIFE.

And because Christ is our light, He is also our life. As in the natural world, so in the spiritual, light and life are not so much twain as one. Let us therefore pursue our line of thought as it leads us to

CHRIST OUR LIFE.

For the Christ-life is the one and only true life of man; and he who knows not this life is not really and fully alive. This Christ-life is ideal man-life. Remember life, man's life, is more than mere self-conscious existence. Life is a thing of *kind* and of *degree*, ranging in the physical realm from the simplest bioplast in its infinitesimal cell up to the complex, marvellous anatomy of man: and in the mental, moral and spiritual realms, from the shallow-brained, untutored savage up to the genius of a Shakespeare or Milton.

The Astronomer Newton and his little dog "Diamond" were both alive: but who would dream that both were living the same life? To the dog, life was a narrow round of sensations and impulses, and probably but little more. He could roam through the lanes and meadows with his master, but he could not roam with him, through the infinite, starry heavens; nor track, with Newton, the windings of the "milky-way" as it stretches its awful amplitudes through space. No: dog-life is not man-life; though some men degrade themselves below the level of the brute.

Equally wide of the mark are they who treat life as if man were a highly organized and refined animal—nothing more. Refine his tastes, control his appetites, educate his higher instincts, as his love of harmony and beauty—meet all his *sensuous* needs—and there is no more *man* left to be cared for! For after all, man is only a superior order of brute. Someone has said that "Man shall not live by bread alone"—but that is an error, you have only to be skilful in the making and baking of your bread—that is all! So they seem to think.

Alas for the degradingly low ideals of this mammon-cursed age. We will pull down our barns and build greater. We will join in the general helter-skelter to the gold and diamond mines. We will vulgarise our sons by teaching them that money is the one end of life, and that they must spend themselves to grasp it; we will sell our daughters at the markets to the highest bidders, and cry " this is life!"

No: no: such possessions are not life.

Life is nobility of soul, purity of heart, a spirit overflowing with love, ceaseless activity in well-doing, the peace of mind that passeth all understanding, a conscience void of offence before God and man—in a word CHRIST within—this, this is *life:* and he who is thus alive lives more in five minutes, than the Christless man in fifty

THE LIGHT OF LIFE.

years. "He that hath the Son hath life, and he that hath not the Son hath not life."

For there are but two kinds of life possible to men, the self-centred and the Christ-centred; and the former of these is not life but death. Of all things under the sun nothing is meaner or more pitiable than it, for it is the saddest travesty of life—hollow and dead. O, to live the life of "overflow from self;" the fuller, deeper, sweeter Christ-life.

"A heart at leisure from itself,
To sooth and sympathize."

Then Christ would be to us life's grandest reality: not one of its joys, but its *one* joy; not one light amongst many which may be extinguished without sensibly darkening our path, but the one LIGHT OF LIFE whose going out would leave us in the night of despair.

"Christ in you," this is "the hope of glory," this the *sweet soul of life,* that, like the oft-recurring refrain of some grand chorus, runs through all the mingled notes and endless melodies, harmonizing and sustaining all. Nor did we know what music slept within our soul till He touched us : we were as organs with our richest tones all silent till the Master-Musician pulled out the stops and swept His fingers over the keys. And now we understand the meaning and feel the force of S. Paul's striking words—" I live ; yet not I, Christ liveth in me."

But because Christ is our light and life He is therefore our loveliness ; and still following the same train of thought we are led up to

Christ our Loveliness.

Now we remember that, in the natural world, light is the soul of beauty ; and all colours reside and blend in the pure white light. It is light's soft, wondrous brush that lays on all those infinite shades of hue and colour which robe the world in loveliness. It is light that paints so exquis-

THE LIGHT OF LIFE.

itely the lilies of the field and clothes them in attire so glorious, that "Solomon in all his glory was not arrayed like one of these." It is light that sets a mitre of silver on the brows of age, mantles the cheek of lovely, blooming youth, and sheds an aureola of gold around the head of fair and happy childhood. Light is God's free gift to the world, and is the exhaustless fountain of all outward and visible beauty.

Even so, Christ is the fountain of soul-loveliness, and there is nothing so beautiful on earth or in Heaven as SOUL-BEAUTY. Wherever there is a soul pure and lovely, that is Christ's work, just as truly as the flower is born of the light. The pure, the chivalrous, the gentle, with the light of Heaven on their brows, are so beautiful because they are full of Christ, and are robed with His loveliness. They think as He thinks, feel as He feels, will as He wills, love as He loves. They drink of His cup, are baptised with His baptism, and in their measure reflect the same glory. Already they are like Him, and one day they shall be still more like Him, for they "shall see Him as He is."

This transformation from the image of the earthy to the image of the heavenly—from self to Christ, is now going on; for we are being changed from glory to glory. In Nature, light mingles with and subtly controls the myriad transformations of growing plant and opening flower: but in that still more wondrous realm of human life, thought, and love, there is a higher Light for ever vitalizing, transforming, and beautifying the Soul; and that Light is CHRIST.

.   .   .   .   .   .

It was a glorious May morning when the Sun rose in a sky without a cloud, and shone upon the world. The birds broke into song; and all around, on leaf and blade of grass, hung myriads of dew-drops glittering in the Sun. What untold wealth of diamonds! And in

THE LIGHT OF LIFE.

every crystal drop an image of the Sun Himself.

O, let us open our souls to the Sun of Righteousness, and His image will shine in our lives.

Come, oh Thou *Light,* and *Life,* and *Loveliness* of men—Redeemer and Lover of us all—come shine away our sin.

THE LIGHT OF LIFE.

LIFE-GIVING LIGHT.

All, all was still and silent;
Across the sky dark mantles hung,
And birds their evening songs had sung
   Before Night's dusky reign.

The moon rose o'er the mountain,
And suddenly a shining stream
Like molten silver, in a dream,
   Shone down its emerald side.

And there 'mid peaks of granite,
A sparkling opal lakelet lay,
Fast caught and held in craggy sway
   Below the gleaming crests.

Again the heavy curtains!
Dark clouds appear,
Tho' greyer now and misty,
For Day is near!

THE LIGHT OF LIFE.

Behold, the sun has risen!
And darkened meads are brilliant green
Bestarred with purple crocus sheen,
    Among the jewelled blades.

The little flower fast sleeping
Beneath the evening's drowsy shade
Smiles not, nor opens to the glade
    Her cup of dazzling gold.

For Dark is ever blind and sad,
    But Light is ever bright,
And calls the flowers, the lakes, the streams
    From out the gloomy Night.

Oh! Christ, shine on our darkened souls,
    And speed our night away;
Oh! lead us thro' the valley, Lord,
    Up, up to endless Day!

                        H. M. C.

UNFINISHED TOWERS.
(RETROSPECTIVE.)

" This man began to build and was not able to finish." S. LUKE 14 C., 30 V.

THOUGH every man's life comes to an end at last, yet how rarely is a life *completed*. We end our lives, but do not finish them. When what has been is regarded in the light of what might have been, a sense of incompleteness, not to say failure, haunts the best and noblest minds; for the past affords them less ground for self-congratulation than for regret if not reproach.

Few indeed are they who can truly say they have done all that it was their duty to do: but beyond all words thrice happy she who gained

UNFINISHED TOWERS.

the grand eulogium of the Master—"She hath done *what she could*"!

As in certain parts of the Globe night falls swiftly upon the workman, and darkness stops the hand still busy with the unfinished work, so comes the last darkness upon us, and we lie down to die feeling how little we have accomplished, and how much has been left undone. True, it was permitted one rare spirit to say,—",I have fought a good fight, I have finished my course;"—but even S. Paul found so little satisfaction in retrospect that he did not count himself to have "apprehended," but declares the law of his life to be *oblivion of the past* by filling mind and hands with the next duty—this one thing I do, "forgetting those things which are behind, and reaching forth unto those things which are before, I press toward the mark . . . "

Of all the sons of men, One only—the Son of Man, the unique Servant of Heaven, has been

UNFINISHED TOWERS.

able to say at the portals of death, "I have FINISHED the work which Thou gavest me to do;" and again—" It is FINISHED."

It is far otherwise with us. We look back at life's pathway winding its devious track over hill and dale, by city and village, town and hamlet, smiling plains and barren wastes, only to realize with humiliation and pain, that the road is too clearly marked by the half-built towers which we began to build but left unfinished.

Those schemes which we took up with so much ardour and dropped with so much haste: those plans of earlier years adopted with glowing enthusiasm, and cast aside at the first difficulties we met. Those high hopes, born and cherished by a fond and vain ambition, vanishing at the first touch of life's prosaic, cold reality, like dreams at dawn. Those resolutions so impulsively though sincerely formed, and so quickly forgotten and lost to sight like the neg-

UNFINISHED TOWERS.

lected foundations of towers,—*weed-overgrown*. Those vows we made on bended knees, with tears and sighs, and broke at the first temptation, almost before our tears were dry and the wounds of our former sorrow healed. Those forms of active service for Christ, in which for a time none more busy or more happy than we, but which we gave up because this present world grew upon us as the years grew, and the powers of the world to come loosened their hold over our sordid spirits. Such are the unfinished towers along life's sorrowful retrospect; and it is poor consolation to reflect that, after all, we have done *some* good, and that our life has not been altogether in vain.

True, it may comfort us to know that at least one man owes his glad life to us, and that we have saved him from the whirlpool in which his brothers have gone down—but if we feel that we might have saved his brothers too, the heart of our joy is struck through.

UNFINISHED TOWERS.

Or, perchance, this backward glance at life's unfinished towers may touch us with tenderer pathos still, as the light of memory softly falls on those dear friendships of long ago,—proud towers our loved and we had begun to build when death's swift night descending stopped their hands, while as yet the walls were only beginning to rise. But of these towers what matters? Will they not go on rising when the morning breaks? and have we not all Eternity in which to build?

Nor will this glance backward be lost in useless regrets if it spur us to fresh effort while yet so much remains to be accomplished.

For life's retrospect does not stretch across the landscape only in shadow and gloom.

There are towers there shining in the warm sunlight beautifully complete; towers whose foundation-stones our hands almost, perhaps quite unconsciously laid, but which the hands of other men and of angels have gloriously finished.

And, for the rest,—"He knoweth our frame; He remembereth that we are *dust;*" and our work will be judged not only by what we have done or by what we have failed to accomplish, but also by what we MEANT to do.

Another consideration should check our rising despondency and re-inforce our hope and courage. *We* are not the final judges of our success or failure. In the graphic, awe-inspiring picture of the last judgment, drawn by our Lord, nothing is more striking, one might add more startling, than the simple, *unconscious* goodness of those selected for the Divine approbation and reward. None more surprised than they who received the "Come ye blessed of my Father." They appear to have been absolutely ignorant of the real character of their deeds; and the judgment pronounced upon those deeds at the great Throne startled them into what was

UNFINISHED TOWERS.

almost a denial of their authorship! *Is not our unconscious influence the truer and greater part of our personality?* And may we not believe that there are social, moral, and spiritual forces at work in the world, in ten thousand ways of which we cannot dream, which owe their origin to us? Perchance there are men, women, and little children bravely fighting, nobly living, patiently suffering, fervently praying, and joyfully climbing Heavenward—all because we have lived.

Neither did we leave *all* life's towers half finished. What of those undertakings conscientiously pursued till every duty pertaining to them had been faithfully discharged? What of those long years of patient endurance and quiet suffering while only He who permitted the weary burden could measure the heroism that bore the daily cross? And what again of that unceasing toil for the Master, so palpably and visibly rewarded, and of which it would be both weak and wrong to doubt the Heaven-blest issues?

UNFINISHED TOWERS.

And yet—and yet, who is not conscious that these towers also were never finished as we meant them to be? The ideal tower was tall, stately, of polished stones perfectly cut and fitted, and rose before us grandly symmetrical—all fair and beautiful within and without. How disappointingly different from the ideal is the real tower. As we think of it, with its unnumbered blemishes and imperfections, we turn to the Divine Mercy with the prayer in our hearts,—

"What I have done
May He, within Himself, make pure!"

Then, too, are there not some towers *happily* left unfinished?—towers concerning which our only regret is that we ever began to build them? From these records of our waywardness and folly we turn away, casting ourselves upon the Infinite Love. If there have been days and nights when, following our caprices or yielding to our selfish impulses, we have gone fishing only to waste life's precious strength in toiling hard and catching

UNFINISHED TOWERS.

nothing, what can we now do but take refuge, as Peter did, in the dear heart of Him who, meeting us in the morning of a brighter day, is calling us again to fellowship with Him. "Lord Thou knowest all things—Thou knowest that I love Thee."

But, for the love of Christ and men, let us go on with the good work to which we have put our hands. What if the tower does not seem to rise so strong, and fair and fast as we had hoped? *No man knows all the good he is doing.* That man tending the lamps in yonder light-house knows that he is doing a good work, but he cannot know how many of his brothers out there in the storm and night will live to hail the break of day again, because he is at his post of duty.

Therefore let us work on with both hands while yet the hours last, remembering that—

UNFINISHED TOWERS.

" For the building that we raise
    Time is with material filled,
Our to-days and yesterdays
    Are the blocks with which we build."

. .   .

As to the results of our poor, individual toil, we shall know them on the great Day, the Day of days, but not till then.

A poor sculptor who had grown foot-sore and heart-weary searching for work, at length found employment on a Cathedral then building. He was taken to a small back shed and given a block of marble, with instructions to carve upon it an angel's face. Day after day he laboured at his task till it was finished; and then this unknown sculptor went his way. Long afterwards he returned to the town, and on passing by the now finished Cathedral, saw, with glad surprise, his own angel looking down upon him from the grand façade of the glorious pile!

UNFINISHED TOWERS.

Now—" Many that are first shall be last ; and the last shall be FIRST."

UNFINISHED TOWERS.

HALF-BUILT TOWERS.

All along life's solemn pathway
    Darkness lowers,
As sad mem'ry strikes a light on
    Half-built towers.

Towers with hope and pride constructed
    Long ago,
But before the noon had lengthened—
    All laid low!

Some were carved; rich buds of promise
    Clustered round,
Till a storm-wind threw them lightly
    To the ground!

Others rose in heightened splendour
    To the sky,
When an earth-shock rudely hurled them
    From on high!

UNFINISHED TOWERS.

One was girt with flowery garlands
    On the sand;
Then the waves of time and tempest
    Claimed the land!

So the towers of hope—ambition
    Sadly fall,
For we *tire*, and leave unfinished
    Duties all!

Try our best to do for Christ's sake,
    Tho' 'tis frail,
He will judge us by our *meaning*
    If we fail.

For the Christ who died and suffered
    For us here,
Gently whispers when He calls us—
    "Never fear!"

Then take heart and rear our towers
    Once again,
Till the Heavenly music bids us
    Join the strain.

                    H. M. C.

THE COMPASSIONATE CHRIST.

" He was moved with Compassion."

MATTHEW 9 C., 36 V.

THERE were two sights which made Jesus weep; one was the City—the other the Grave.

On the one hand throbbing, eager, feverish life; and on the other cold, still death.

Life with its mingled lights and shadows—joys and sorrows, dreams and disillusions—its pathos of laughter and tears, its tragedy of sin and suffering; and death with its silence and mystery.

THE COMPASSIONATE CHRIST.

Over the Mammon-ridden, self-seeking City that would not or could not weep for itself, Jesus wept; and when He stood face to face with real grief by the grave of His friend, He could not keep back His tears.

Now this beautiful compassion is the charm of Jesus; this it is which draws all hearts to Him. Men want sympathy, comfort, pardon, rest; and the world's keenest hunger is its hunger for LOVE. This hunger Jesus satisfies.

If you would understand the attraction of Christ, think of His compassion. For this explains why dear little children came running to Him, laughing through their tears and looking up for His smile. Flowers sweet with morning dew kissed by the sun.

This also it was, and not His miracles, that drew around Him lost men and wretched women, with every chord of life snapped save the one

THE COMPASSIONATE CHRIST.

chord that trembled at the touch of *love*. They felt that "back of His strength lay His compassion, His tears;" they knew that behind His mighty power was the golden secret—"Behold how He loved him."

The great miracle—the miracle of miracles—is not the raising of the dead, but the forgiveness of sins. Not the raising of a dead body, but the quickening of a dead soul.

Nor is there any feature of that Sublime Personality more lovely or more attractive than the Redeemer's compassion. And what is compassion? Love touched with pity—it is love *stooping*. "I am among you as one that serveth."

How subtle the blending of majesty with humility, of strength with gentleness, of passion with repose, of perfect holiness with sympathy for sinful, sorrowing men. Like some Alpine range its snow-peaks in heaven inaccessible to

THE COMPASSIONATE CHRIST.

human feet, while yet its sunny slopes and green valleys are the shelter and the home of men.

Jesus is unique ; *the* Son of Man.

Ernest Renan was right when he wrote that whatever surprises the future may bring, " in any case Jesus will never be surpassed." So high, so lowly ; so great, so tender ; so far away and yet so near.

"Thou seemest human and divine."

Charles Lamb was once conversing with friends as to how they would feel were certain of the illustrious dead suddenly to appear. One said "And if Christ were to enter this room?" With abrupt change of manner Lamb stammered out "—you see—if Shakespeare entered we should all rise—but if Christ appeared we must *kneel.*"

Conscious as we are of His infinite strength

THE COMPASSIONATE CHRIST.

and Majesty, we feel too that He is not a high priest who "cannot be touched with the feeling of our infirmities."

Christ's compassion is God's love in a human heart—that Love which arches over all our life like a Rainbow from sky to sky.

. . . . . .

In considering this suggestive theme let us observe first that—

THE COMPASSION OF JESUS OVERFLOWED TOWARDS YOUNG LIFE.

I love to think of Him as for ever young. In the early prime of manhood He died. No touch of withering age was ever upon Him. In the poetic imagery of Solomon's Song, our Beloved is ruddy of countenance and His locks are black as a raven.

Immortal youth and beauty belong to Jesus.

THE COMPASSIONATE CHRIST.

His sympathy with childhood is most refreshing and beautiful. The merry children touched Him to the quick, thrilling and charming Him. They were so bright, free, unrestrained and unconventional; so artless, transparent, natural and sincere; so far removed from the greed, anxiety, hollowness and guile of the world, that with the little ones He was simply at home. It was as if He and they away from the same home had met in a foreign land. They filled His heart with joy, drawing from Him some of His tenderest words, as the gentle zephyr wakes the sweetest tones of the Æolian harp.

How wonderful are His words on the children! How enthusiastic and passionate His defence of them; how scathing the denunciations poured from those gentlest of lips against any offenders of the young.

Did not His eyes flash fire when the little ones were kept back from Him? It was the

THE COMPASSIONATE CHRIST.

wrath of the Lamb. Like lightning in the summer sky.

Dr. G. MacDonald somewhere says we ought never to tell a child that he has a soul but that "he *is* a soul and has a body." A *lovely character* is more than all else.

The quickening of the public conscience, in this regard, is one of the best signs of our onward march, as bear witness the unnumbered agencies now at work for the preservation and salvation of young life. Here join hands all remedial forces, Religious, Social, and Political.

Nor can the mind fathom half the depth of tender love in the heart of the Great Shepherd who carrieth the lambs in His bosom.

Mr. George Sims has pictured, with a touch of true pathos, the little street arab as he lay dying, listening eagerly to his sister's description

THE COMPASSIONATE CHRIST.

of Jesus and Heaven.

"Then she told some garbled story of a kind-eyed Saviour's love,
How He'd built for little children, great, big playgrounds up above,
Where they sang and played at hopscotch and at horses all the day,
And where beadles and policemen never frightened them away.

This was Nell's idea of Heaven—just a bit of what she'd heard,
With a little bit invented, and a little bit inferred,
But her brother lay and listened and he seemed to understand,
For he closed his eyes and murmured he could see the Promised Land."

Surely it is the children's Jesus moving behind and through all our modern agencies for the salvation of childhood; surely it is He "the same yesterday, to-day and for ever," who is thus

THE COMPASSIONATE CHRIST.

gathering the little ones beneath the warm wings of His compassion, as a hen gathereth her brood.

Never forget how hungry for love, for sympathy, for encouragement, for just a touch of kindness the children always are.

" In the two twilights of childhood and age tears fall most easily, like the dew at dawn and eve."

Be sure it is the highest of all Voices which is saying to Legislators, to Christian Ministers and their flocks, to Employers of labour, to Magistrates, to Town and County Councils, to Poor Law Guardians, to School Boards, to our great public schools, to parents, to one and all : " Whoso shall offend one of these little ones which believe in Me, it were better for him that a mill-stone were hanged about his neck, and that he were drowned in the depth of the sea !"

THE COMPASSIONATE CHRIST.

Who does not feel the intense passion throbbing in this utterance of the Master? Who can look upon this bush ablaze with God and vocal with Love, and not be conscious that he is standing upon holy ground?

"Suffer the little children to come unto me," *suffer* them to come. That is—see that you do not stand between the child and Christ.

It was Charles Dickens who wrote of children :—

"I taught them the goodness of knowledge,
They taught me the goodness of God!"

But observe secondly that—

THE COMPASSION OF JESUS WAS STIRRED BY THE MULTITUDE.

It was when He faced the fainting multitude that "He was moved with compassion:" it was

THE COMPASSIONATE CHRIST.

when He came near to the city, and beheld it, that He broke down.

Ah—the city with all its sin, sorrow, shame! The city with its eager rivalries, vain ambitions, petty jealousies, degrading bestiality; its hard-visaged toil and harder-hearted Mammonism. Hopeful, struggling, broken hearts—abode of labour, sweat and blood.

Here breaks life's blushing dawn; here too burns life's sultry noon; and here is bent old age with no light at eventide.

Who that knows Jesus can wonder that He wept over the city?

It was the city that cried " Hosanna :" it was the city that raised the Cross. It was the city that the Redeemer twice baptized, first with tears and then with blood.

THE COMPASSIONATE CHRIST.

And where is "the city?" In Palestine? No! Wherever men congregate—there is the city.

The Saviour and the multitude still stand face to face.

The gravest problem before us to-day is—the multitude—what to do with it, and how best to do it?

I think that a wiser generation than ours, understanding better the handwriting on Nature's wall of inviolable law, will avoid much suffering, in which the ignorance of the past and present now entangles us. A little more knowledge, with wisdom to apply it, will mean much less suffering: and it is about as reasonable to link the Almighty with half the world's pain, as to blame Him for the window tax and its evil consequences!

But were I to say that knowledge is in itself

THE COMPASSIONATE CHRIST.

salvation, ten thousand facts of life patent to all would refute me. The man who *knows* is often the greatest offender. The solution of the problem lies much deeper. There is something more behind. "Except a man be born again he cannot see the Kingdom of God."

You cannot make a strong chain with rotten links: you cannot evoke a virtuous social order from impure hearts.

You may expect a regenerate society when you get regenerate *men*—till then your expectation is a baseless dream. Jesus knew this: hence His great patience with individuals.

For the moment, however, let us observe Him facing the multitudes.

Who can describe the mingled feelings that rise within us as we face a great crowd? The crowd is more than a collection of units,

THE COMPASSIONATE CHRIST.

as the river is something more than a number of individual drops. The crowd is life multiplied and *intensified;*—few sights can thrill one so strangely as a great sea of human faces.

It is said that Xerxes wept like a child as he gazed upon his fighting hosts, for he reflected that very soon they would all be no more.

But deeper feelings than these stirred the Son of Man as he faced the multitude. He knew their weariness of body and of mind, their toil for the bread that perishes, their stumblings in the darkness and their gropings after the light of Life. He understood their irrepressible cries for a deeper peace than earth can give, their constant unrest upon life's troubled sea. He knew their frailty: He saw in them "the bruised reed, the smoking flax"—but in His eyes their very grief was sacred, their helplessness an appeal to His pity.

THE COMPASSIONATE CHRIST.

They were frail, yet of untold worth; they were "bruised" but still capable of God-like beauty and strength. He thought of that wealth of love in their bosoms frittered away—a river intended to fertilize the world yet pouring its precious waters into the salt wastes of the dead sea.

It was the world's waste of love that appalled Jesus.

To Him it was the prodigal wasting his substance for the husks and the famine.

Nor must we fail to mark this cardinal point—the compassion of Jesus was not mere sentiment but sacrifice. He began both to feed and to teach.

A lady stood in the Academy before a masterpiece weeping at the artist's representation of a starving child : but she had no gift for the hungry little waif who gazed wistfully at her as she entered her carriage. Her feelings were mere sentiment; and sentiment void of sympathy is a well without water. Whatever else it may be it is not Christian. Christian compassion begins at once to feed and to teach. Wherever it discovers darkness it rises upon it, like the sun, with healing in his wings.

And in service for others—service which means *self-giving*—lies the true Christ-life : here and nowhere else.

Our duty includes indeed, signing of cheques, giving of gold and silver—but that will never save the world. In a very deep sense one may say—"without shedding of *blood* there is no remission." Do you remember that although the prophet sent his servant with the staff the child still lay cold and dead ? It was not until Elisha himself came and breathed his own life into the stiffened form that the warm blush of life returned

THE COMPASSIONATE CHRIST.

to the lad, and gladness came back to that home.

If you would work the miracle—give *yourself*.

There is another point which must not escape us. It has already been hinted at. Jesus did not see only the multitude in the crowd. It is the stranger who sees "the family:" the Mother knows each child as though she had no other. Each one forms a special study and is her peculiar care.

Love individualises and discriminates; and this is the beautiful paradox of her arithmetic that to divide is not to diminish but to multiply! It is like the light which every flower in the valley may claim for its very own.

There was not one in all that fainting multitude for whom Jesus would not have died. He who forgot thirst and weariness in earnest

THE COMPASSIONATE CHRIST.

talk with an unhappy woman, the bloom of whose beauty had passed; who found time in the midst of a busy day to turn aside to where the little maid lay, and wake her from that marble sleep; who invited Himself to the house of a man who was in the public opinion "a sinner," because He knew the good that was in him; who gave the keys of authority to the very man that had denied Him; and who amidst the agonies of crucifixion remembered that His mother was homeless, is just the Saviour we need—One who is " touched with the feeling of our infirmities."

For Jesus sees not the crowd merely—but *men*.

It is a crude philosophy that talks of the classes and the masses. You cannot classify and label men as a chemist his bottles! Every new life is a fresh experiment: every child an unsolved problem: every man is unique.

THE COMPASSIONATE CHRIST.

The eye of Jesus looked through the coating of veneer to the real man underneath. He saw far down beneath the surface waters, the bottom of mud or of pearls. Hence a poor wretch, with no sympathy but the lick of dumb dogs, bulked before Him a much grander man than Dives in his luxury. Beneath the purple of a king He saw only a "fox," while under the shabby attire of a pauper widow His glance detected the queen of philanthropists!

"Never man spake like this man."

Let us pass on to observe finally, that—

THE COMPASSION OF JESUS TOUCHED AND SANCTIFIED THE HOME CIRCLE.

One feels how highly privileged was that home at Bethany, where the Master appears so frequently to have rested; the home with which, above all others, His name is now for ever linked.

THE COMPASSIONATE CHRIST.

How great the privilege of the meditative Mary as she sat at His feet, drinking in His love, and listening to His talk as to the music of Heaven: how highly honoured was Martha in preparing the food so necessary for His body—that body which had grown weary in doing only good. And how intensely Jesus loved both their brother and them. But what glorious recompense for their devotion to Him did they receive in the thought that *they belonged to His circle of friends*.

I do not know if you have ever thought over that strikingly beautiful remark dropped incidentally by the Master—" our friend Lazarus sleepeth "—our *friend*. Who was this " friend." What had he done to be included within the golden circle of Christ's friendship? Was he a Prophet? No. An Apostle? No. A great public disciple and follower of the Nazarene? No: No: nothing of the kind. *Simply a quiet man in a quiet home*. A type of the many

THE COMPASSIONATE CHRIST.

friends of Jesus whose influence is for the home-circle. To one was said "follow Me;" but to another "go home and tell thy friends."

There is no sphere of influence comparable to a sweet home, nò sanctuary like it!

What kind of man Lazarus was, we may guess from the passionate grief of the sisters— the two good women who mourned his loss. How much of their life he formed, and how much of it he absorbed, they had not realized till now —now that the death of their loved one had left the world empty and cold.

The story of the trouble that overshadowed this favoured home is full of pathos. Death knocking at the door while the Master of Life was away. Then His coming when it was too late—too late for all but Jesus. Why did He not come while the precious life trembled in the balance—why prolong the agony of the sisters?

THE COMPASSIONATE CHRIST.

Why did He not come till suspense had sunk in despair? No—not quite despair. What could be finer than Martha's tremulous hope sobbed out with broken words, "I know—that even now—whatsoever thou wilt ask of God—God will give it thee."

Blest faith that can thus lay her hand upon the exhaustless stores of the Divine Love, and can say when all seems lost,—" I know that even now." Beyond the Night the gates of the Morning! After our brother's death, the special coming to us of the Saviour with the sublime words of comfort, — "thy brother shall rise again;" and then His gracious Presence at the grave-side, not rebuking us for our grief, but mingling His warm tears with ours.

Jesus wept and Lazarus awoke—new life after the sweet spring rains. There is a Love stronger than death, a Friend that sticketh closer than a brother: and His sympathy so human,

THE COMPASSIONATE CHRIST.

so divine, is ours still. Of this crystal stream we are drinking every day. It flows from the divine man who was wounded for our transgressions—the Rock that was smitten for us—and that Rock is Christ. For all in whom He fully dwells are filled to overflowing with His compassion.

Do not believe the cold scepticism that says this Holy Thing is gone. A thousand times ten thousand—No! It is here in our very midst to-day. Divine Love incarnate now in every heart where Jesus dwells, and shedding upon earth a light from Heaven.

It lingers like a halo around the whitened brows of age—the grandfather or grandmother at home: it shines like a beacon-light from the stormier years of manhood's prime and womanhood's maturity, the strong father—the patient mother: it flashes from the laughing heart of childhood as sunlight from the summer sea.

THE COMPASSIONATE CHRIST.

"The dear Lord's best interpreters
   Are humble, human souls;
The Gospel of a life like hers
   Is more than books and scrolls.

From scheme and creed the light goes out;
   The saintly fact survives:
The Blessed Master none can doubt
   Revealed in human lives."

Yet the light that only gleams so faintly in us shines from Him with full-orbed glory.

Even upon the Cross, amidst the thick shadows of death and of the darkness that shrouded Calvary, this beautiful compassion broke from Him as the setting sun through a dense bank of clouds. It lighted upon His murderers for whom He prayed; it lingered for one brief moment about that form, bent with grief, standing close to the Cross. "Woman, behold thy son" —then said He to the disciple whom He loved, "Behold thy mother."

THE COMPASSIONATE CHRIST.

And are *you* a disciple whom Jesus loves?

Then know that to you the Master is saying of every little child vexed with pain and grief, " behold thy child ;" of every poor woman bent with sorrow, " behold thy mother."

This is the Saviour I love to preach. No far-away Deity throned in unapproachable splendours, but the God-Man — Christ Jesus who blessed little children, who healed broken hearts, who gave to lost men and women a fresh chance in life, who broke down at the sight of the city, who wept for very pity by His friend's grave, who baptized the world with His tears and with His blood.

" Behold the Lamb of God that taketh away the sin of the world."

You cannot fail to recognize Him. On Earth beneath, in Heaven above there is none like Him.

THE COMPASSIONATE CHRIST.

"In His feet and hands are wound-prints
And His side."

BELLS OF PURE GOLD.
(FOR THE YOUNG.)
"*Bells of Pure Gold.*" EXODUS 39 C., 25 V.

A BRIEF glance at the context will show in what connection these words occur.

They refer to the garments of the high-priest, and, in particular, to the fringe of golden bells and imitation pomegranates " upon the robe of the ephod all of blue ;" a colour suggestive of Heaven. Now these bells, ringing when Aaron went " in unto the holy-place before the Lord," awaken many thoughts within the mind as we listen to their melody. For the human heart, like the tabernacle of old, has its outer and inner

BELLS OF PURE GOLD.

places ; and these bells may serve to remind us that our Great High Priest, Christ Jesus, when He enters the sanctuary of our heart, brings with Him the harmonies of Heaven.

He comes into the soul as with the ringing of sweet bells. Loud bells, soft bells, glad bells, sorrowful bells ; rousing us, soothing us, filling us with sorrow yet making us glad. Let us now listen to the ringing of some of these bells of pure gold.

Bells of *Conviction, Contrition, Conversion, Confession, Consecration, Consistency, Consolation, Conquest.*

And first let us listen to the

BELL OF CONVICTION.

The ringing of this solemn bell in the soul is, our Lord tells us, the work of the Holy Spirit (John 16 c. 7 to 11 v.). The Paraclete, the Exhorter, speaking now in the "still small voice," and now in tones of thunder, awakens the conscience to the deep and awe-inspiring realities —"sin, righteousness and judgment to come." At the ringing of this bell the soul is thrilled with grief and shame, and the prayer of the publican trembles on the lips—"God be merciful to me a sinner." O it is a solemn moment in life when the pointed personal conviction of sin alarms the soul—for that moment full often holds in it the issues of life and death. This is *God's alarm bell.*

When the voice of a violated and accusing conscience is heard within; when the sin committed haunts us day and night like an awful dream from which there is no awakening; when the wrong that we have done calls aloud like Abel's blood from the ground and will not be silenced; when the guilty deed rises before the mind,—a ghost that cannot rest—crying "*Thou art the man,*" then God's alarm bell is ringing,

BELLS OF PURE GOLD.

and the soul cowers like a guilty thing, trembling and undone. "And David said unto Nathan I have sinned against the Lord."

Who is bold enough to go one step further when Conscience stands like the angel before Balaam, with drawn sword to keep the way?

"Thus conscience doth make cowards of us all."

When the revealing light falls upon the wall and the mysterious hand is seen tracing its letters of fire, the godless and dissolute king is sorely troubled at the sight, but that night ere the effects of his debauchery have left him his life is taken. —(Daniel 5 c. 30 v.)

It is, however, a sorrowful truth that multitudes who undergo all the penitential feelings just described, yet continue in their sin. Like the poor, silly moth, whose wings are already singed, they play with the flame till it destroys them. They tremble but they do not repent. Felix is alarmed but that is all : he does not forsake his wicked life, and Drusilla is still his companion. It is not enough to be alarmed because of our sin, for unless there is true repentance and a turning away from the course of shame, the ringing of this golden bell will be to us only a "savour of death unto death."

Recollect how differently under similar impressions the Philippian jailer acted. At the sound of this bell he fell upon his knees crying—"What must I do to be saved." To him it was "the savour of life unto life."

Over many a sunken wreck floats a buoy with a bell upon it. By night and by day the danger signal rings out its warning notes, as the waves rock the buoy to and fro. Over many a wicked and ruined life the solemn bell tolls—"The wages of sin is DEATH." If you value your eternal interests do not turn a deaf ear to this warning bell. But possibly some may feel that such a deep sense of conviction has never been theirs, and that, therefore, they are not the subjects of the Holy Spirit's gracious visitations. This is, surely, a very common mistake. "The chariots of God are *twenty thousand.*"

For Paul the blinding light, and for Luther the lightning flash; but for Timothy the sweet influences of pious training, and for Lydia, that quiet opening of the heart as of a flower unfolding in the morning sun.

To natures like Timothy's and Lydia's the Holy Spirit first reveals the loveliness and lovableness of Jesus. And this is but another side of the same work, for he who feels the purity of Christ is sure to feel by contrast his own sinfulness. There is no loftier conception of Christ's majesty, purity, and loveliness than that presented by the glowing pen of S. Paul, yet no one has depicted in truer words the personal conviction of sin. If

BELLS OF PURE GOLD.

you love Christ do not be alarmed because you have never wept like Mary or trembled like Felix; for to many a loving soul the ringing of this golden bell is soft as the music of æolian harps, and gentle as the cooing of a dove.

And this reminds us of another bell which rings in the soul when Jesus is within its most holy place; it is the

BELL OF CONTRITION.

For where there is true conviction there will speedily follow deep contrition, unless, indeed, we are guilty of quenching the Holy Spirit. Sweet is the sound of this bell in the Father's ear. "The sacrifices of God are a broken spirit."

As we read the fifty-first Psalm, we hear, all through it, the ringing of this trembling bell. What sorrow for sin, what yearning after purity and peace, what holy fear lest the Divine Spirit forsake him, what heartfelt longings after the lost

BELLS OF PURE GOLD.

joy, what prayers for help and guidance, what promises of future usefulness!

At the ringing of this solemn bell, kneel and pray; and let the cry of penitence thrill your heart also,—"take not Thy Holy Spirit from me."

But recollect there are two kinds of sorrow for sin. There is the sorrow that brings in a new life, and there is the sorrow that sheds tears but does not forsake the sin. Draw the line sharp and clear between Contrition and Remorse. Peter's was true Contrition, for it wrought in him such glorious results, an after-life of unfaltering fidelity and unquenchable zeal; but the grief of Judas was the bitter remorse of a self-accusing conscience—a sorrow that drew him not to Christ, but drave him to suicide. It was the sorrow that worketh death. His sun set in a sky of lead, with scarce a single ray of soft light or a solitary opening of blue. Alas, for human life when hope has fled, and the destroying angel of Despair haunts the soul. Now, contrast Judas with Mary and we pass at once from remorse to contrition.

Remorse sheds tears, but not at the Redeemer's feet: she hides her shame in the solitude of despair, away from men, away from Christ. Remorse breaks no alabaster box and brings no offering of love.

But thou, poor Mary, sin-stained and corrupted, thy name a by-word, thy character gone, thy life a foul confusion of sin and shame, how canst thou come to the pure and sinless One? Memorable lesson of Redeeming love :—that love which, alone, seeks and saves the lost.

There is an old legend that, originally, Church bells were used to ring away evil spirits: and so these bells of Heaven, bells of conviction and contrition, ring away evil spirits

BELLS OF PURE GOLD.

from our hearts, for we begin now to see no glory in the world "by reason of the glory that excelleth."

There are two ways of drowning the tempter's voice. Ulysses stuffed wax in his sailors' ears that the songs of the Sirens might not enchant them, but Meudon overcame the enchantment by sweeter music of his own, and the soul that hears the everlasting harmonies of heaven will, like Moses, turn from the world's fascinations to spiritual joys. O listen to these bells of gold, and they will ring you to the Saviour's feet.

But now another bell begins to ring out its clear notes ; the

BELL OF CONVERSION.

Conviction, Contrition, Conversion, is not this the method of the Holy Spirit ?

BELLS OF PURE GOLD.

There is much misconception in many minds regarding conversion. Conversion really means *a turning* (Acts 11 c. 21 v.). It is the turning of the whole nature away from sin to God. It is the beginning of a new life—it is a change so total and complete that our Lord calls it being "born again." The bearded Nicodemus, though "a master of Israel," cannot enter into the Kingdom of God until this wondrous birth of the Spirit has taken place: and with this new life comes the new nature.

Did you ever, when perhaps alone in your chamber, ask yourself this solemn question—am I born from above? Or in some solitary spot with the silent stars looking down upon you, and with no one to see and to hear you but *Him*—have you ever said, "Lord, Thou knowest all things, Thou knowest that I love Thee."

And if "there is joy in the presence of the angels of God over one sinner that repenteth,"

BELLS OF PURE GOLD.

what gladness must thrill the penitent heart itself like echoes of that joy in Heaven! What feelings must have possessed the dying thief as the sound of these solemn bells, as of music from the stars, broke upon his ears. Amidst the wild, confused mutterings of the crowd, their taunts and sneers mingling in strange manner with his dying agonies and groans, what is this sweet peace that thrills him? Poor reprobate, 'tis the dying, living Saviour who speaks to thee. A very memorable scene! This dying malefactor, too, is convicted of sin, made contrite in soul, and hears the sublime assurance from those sinless lips—" This day thou shalt be with me in Paradise." A sudden conversion, but truly beautiful to a believing, thoughtful soul.

> " Ring the bells of Heaven,
> There is joy to-day."

But conversion is not all: it is only the *beginning* of the new life. The tender green shoot is just bursting its old husk ; air, sunshine and moisture must now do their work. Now the soul should "grow in grace." And most helpful to this spiritual growth is that confession of Christ before men which the Redeemer promises to reward with His own confession before the angels of God (Luke 12 c. 8-9 v.).

This then is the

BELL OF CONFESSION

The multitude of Christ's secret disciples is very great, for as in the days of His earthly sojourn, so now, the fear of man is a terrible hindrance to an open confession of love to the Lord.—(John 12 c. 42-43 v.) Nicodemus and Joseph of Arimathæa are still amongst us ; disciples, indeed they are, but "secretly, for fear." This fear becomes, when yielded to, a galling yoke, and restrains men not only from a confession of Christ, but from taking any steps in respect to Religion which might seem in the slightest degree to commit them. Once conquer your fear and a great moral victory is gained—for he that thus ruleth himself is mightier than he that taketh a city. If you love the Lord, for your own sake confess Him before men. If you stop the ringing of this bell the music of your life will be marred.

Another and yet higher reason for confessing Christ is *the effect of your example.* In such a world as this where soul is linked with soul, and spirit is moulded by spirit, personal influence is a mighty factor. It is one of the mightiest forces in social life. Courage inspires courage. Be courageous for the Master, and your courage may inspire some fearful, trembling soul.

Many are held back from natural modesty: their feeling is that they are not good enough. They imagine that by confessing Christ they are claiming to be better than their neighbours, and being conscious, painfully conscious of their own failings, they do not avow that love they secretly feel. Now, to confess Christ is not to assert our own holiness. It is a confession of our love to Jesus and of our earnest desire to glorify Him. It is an admission that we feel our sinfulness and long to be like Christ. There is, too, a more solemn side to this question, for there are times when " silence is criminal." Not to confess Christ under certain circumstances may be equivalent to denying Him.

Peter's silence, as he sat in the hall there, with the flickering firelight revealing in his face the restlessness of his mind, what was it but the prelude to the spoken denial and the loud impassioned oaths?

We must not be guilty of silencing this golden bell, or, as I have said, the music of our life will be marred and its testimony weakened if not destroyed. Rather let it ring out joyfully every day —" This is my Beloved, and this is my Friend."

BELLS OF PURE GOLD.

And now for one brief moment let us listen to the tones of our next "bell of pure gold:" the

BELL OF CONSECRATION.

Rich and full-toned is the mellow music of this heavenly bell, and its notes enrich the harmony of the peal.

When we are entirely consecrated to Christ the feeling in our heart is, Lord, I am Thine, do with me as Thou wilt. My wealth, health, time, talent, intellect, *will*, all I have and all I am, dear Lord, I give to Thee. "More should'st Thou have if I had more."

Brethren, *the influence of a consecrated life is measureless.* Like the sunbeam that breaks from the golden windows of the East, kindles the snowy mountain peaks into tongues of fire, descends into the valleys and dispels the mists, now lighting up the violet and primrose in the dell, and now turning the rivers into streets of

BELLS OF PURE GOLD.

shining gold—so a life completely consecrated to Christ is an illumining, joy-giving, all-transforming power.

Alas that the worm of *half-heartedness* should gnaw at the root of our joy in Christ, and turn our life into a withered, sapless thing. Let us beware of the subtle sin of Ananias and Sapphira who kept back part of the possession. A half-friend is no friend at all. " I would that thou wert cold or hot."

How beautifully has Miss Frances Ridley Havergal, that sweet songstress of our modern Israel, expressed the spirit of entire surrender to Christ in her " Consecration hymn," and still more strikingly in her consecrated *life*.

O let us keep nothing back from Him who gave *Himself* for us. Though you have only five loaves and two small fishes in your basket yet bring them to the Lord, and the miracle of

BELLS OF PURE GOLD.

multiplication shall be repeated.

By the souls you may win, by the darkened homes you may bless, by the bleeding and broken hearts you may heal, by the fallen you may restore, by the ignorant you may teach, by the little ones you may train, by the sick you may visit, by the starving and naked you may feed and clothe, by the lost that you may save—in a word by all the good that you may do—"I beseech you, therefore, brethren, by the mercies of God, that ye present your bodies a living sacrifice, holy, acceptable unto God, which is your reasonable service." Then will ring the next bell, for a consecrated life is sure to be a consistent one. Therefore, let us now listen to the

BELL OF CONSISTENCY.

For all our fancied consecration is nothing if our lives are inconsistent. Some bells are cracked, and the sound they give grates harshly

BELLS OF PURE GOLD.

on the ear. One cracked bell in a peal is sure to mar the harmony of the whole. It is of little avail to ask for forgiveness if we do not forgive; it is vain to dream we can love and serve God if we do not love and serve our brother.

For our inconsistency is often a fearful stumbling-block to the unconverted. "I know a man, and he is a splendid fellow,—' BUT '—!" Now that "but" is a crack right down the bell. Or "she is a first-rate woman, 'ONLY'—!" Alas, these "buts" and "onlys," would to God we could get rid of them.

A man who lives up to his belief is sure to command respect, even though others differ from his creed. Consistency is power; inconsistency the destruction of all influence for good. Silence this bell and the rest will make but a sorry jingle. Let us beware, however, of charging upon others this failing while we are verily guilty ourselves. Only the truly consistent

BELLS OF PURE GOLD.

may make such a charge, only the absolutely sinless may cast the first stone. We must pull out the beam in our own eye ere we grow so affectionately busy with the mote in our brother's eye. We are sadly ignorant of our own failings, but we bring the microscope to bear on the shortcomings of others.

Now the sweet notes of this bell are charity, love, forgiveness, purity, peace. I have read of a man who had a large rock in his field. "He did not want to waste time and powder to blast and remove it. What did he do? Why he planted ivy and roses and honeysuckles about it to cover it up; and he invites people to come and see how beautiful it is!"

Yes, we plant ivy, roses and honeysuckles to cover our own uglinesses, but we tear away this covering of flowers and examine keenly the naked faults of others. Discontent, ill-temper, selfishness, hatred, envy, and so forth

BELLS OF PURE GOLD.

are so many cracks in the bell, making jarring discords in the music of our life.

As this bell is now sounding in our ears we seem to hear it ringing—"*See that ye love one another with a pure heart fervently.*" Yet "not in word only but in deed and in truth."

BELL OF CONSOLATION.

Now, let us cease our own words and hear this golden bell speaking for itself.

Are you sorrowing for a dear one gone? Hark! "Thy Brother shall rise again!"—so the bell rings.—Are the daisies just growing on a little grave dear to you?—"Of such is the Kingdom of Heaven."—Are you in great suffering, and does the shadow of a broken hope darken your life? Oh, hear this heavenly bell—"Our light afflictions, which are but for a moment, work out for us a far more exceeding and eternal weight of glory." Is your life embittered by some sore trial unknown to the world, and does the daily cross almost make you faint beneath its weary weight?—then listen to this soft, sweet bell—" My grace is sufficient for thee."

Does the present seem to you all dark, and your future a great mystery?—hear, for it rings out gladdest music for you—" All things work together for good to them that love God."

Are you stretched on a bed of pain, the long nights passing with leaden wings, and the fresh morning only seeming to mock your weariness? Oh, let the echoes of this holy bell steal into your ears and comfort your soul—" Thou wilt make all his bed in his sickness," and "underneath are the everlasting arms." " When thou passest through the waters I will be with thee; and through the rivers they shall not overflow thee; when thou walkest through the fire thou shalt not be burned: neither shall the flame kindle upon thee." These are the

BELLS OF PURE GOLD.

consolations of God's children.

In South Wales there is a lake amongst "the Black Mountains" with a small wooded island. A legend says that long ago a Church stood on the island but was swallowed by an earthquake. Yet, now, the natives say that when the storm sweeps down from the mountains and churns the lake into foam, they hear the ringing of the bells. There is music in the true Christian's heart which only trials can awaken, and above the roaring tempest of earth's sorrow the child of God rejoices to hear these golden bells of Heaven.

Then, too, there is the

BELL OF CONQUEST.

The notes of this bell are glad songs of victory. Ring, golden bell !—ring, ring, ring ! Ring out clear and strong in the chambers of the tempted soul " to him that overcometh I will give to sit with me on my throne." "Blessed is the man that *endureth* temptation, for when he is tried he shall receive a crown of life that fadeth not away." "We are more than conquerors through Him that loved us." Is not this joyous music for all the sin-stricken and tempted?— "Be thou faithful unto death and I will give thee a crown of life."

See yonder a road that leads down, down into the shadowy valley. The setting sun falls across the path and lights up the silver hairs of a tired old man.

He is going down into the valley, but through it to the everlasting hills beyond: for the time of his "departure" is at hand. The fight is over, the day is won; and death is swallowed up in victory.

For such faith as Paul's re-christens death, calling it only *departure*—a going to the next

BELLS OF PURE GOLD.

room in the great house of life ; that is all.

Death is not annihilation, but translation, not cessation of being, but only transition.

"Eternal process moving on,
　　From state to state the Spirit walks ;
　　And these are but the shatter'd stalks,
Or ruined chrysalis of one.

Nor blame I Death, because he bare
　　The use of virtue out of earth :
　　I know transplanted human worth
Will bloom to profit, otherwhere."

And what is death to the child of God? It is only *the shadow of life*—as night is but the shadow of day.

The sun is going down, the shadows lengthen, the twilight deepens : the old man is in the valley, but all the bells of Heaven are ringing—" Life, life, eternal life !"

BELLS OF PURE GOLD.

And so, in life and in death, may the Lord sweetly ring all these bells in your soul for His name's sake.

AMEN.

BELLS OF PURE GOLD.

BELLS OF LOVE.

Golden bells of love are chiming,
   Chiming sweet and fair,
With a shout of welcome, pealing,
   Pealing thro' the air.

All the courts of Heaven are ringing,
   Ringing glad and true,
With a happy, joyful singing,
   Singing over *you*.

O'er the soul, that sinking earthwards,
   Ever in the night,
Sees at last the Father's glory
   Wrapt in endless Light.

Hears at last His dear voice speaking
   Words of love and rest,
" Rise ! I give thee peace and pardon,
   Lay thee on My breast !

BELLS OF PURE GOLD.

"Leave the world's sad pomp and grandeur,
   Set thy true self free,
Soothe the sick and broken-hearted,
   Live thy life for Me!"

Yes, the courts of Heaven are ringing,
   Ringing glad and true,
With a happy, joyful singing,
   Singing over *you*.

H. M. C.

CHRIST'S THORN-CROWN.

"A crown of thorns."

MATTHEW 27 C., 29 V.

IF many a true word is spoken in jest, it is equally certain that truth is often uttered with the tongue of irony.

A truth infinitely deeper than those rude soldiers dreamt of underlay the ribald mockery of their "Hail King"; for all unconsciously their blasphemous lips proclaimed the royal majesty of Jesus. Their cry was the cry of Truth extorted from ignorant minds for they knew not what they said. The sovereignty of Christ is the one hope of our sin-stricken world.

CHRIST'S THORN-CROWN.

Observe how strikingly *the silence of Jesus* contrasts with the wild clamours of the excited crowd. He alone of all the multitude is calm and silent, for "as a sheep before her shearers is dumb so He openeth not His mouth." Truth need never be in a hurry, for she can always afford to wait. "In quietness and in confidence shall be your strength," and sooner or later, "wisdom is justified of all her children."

Now to understand this silence of Jesus we have but to look into our own hearts, for there are moments in the most common-place life when emotion hems in all speech, and there are feelings in the commonest heart which lie too deep for words. Even as Nature in her deep self, in her mightiest forces is silent, so our strongest feelings—our deepest griefs and most ecstatic joys—pass into silence. This silence is the soul's sublimest mood and her most eloquent speech.

And thus Jesus forsaken and thorn-crowned,

CHRIST'S THORN-CROWN.

in great bodily pain, crushed down and almost over-whelmed with sorrow sat speechless. *His was the silence of wounded love.*

Let us pause and recall that sad, tragic night and its more tragic morrow. Only a few hours before, He had endured the exhausting soul-agony of Gethsemane, and while the sweat was still upon his brow He had been betrayed by one of His disciples and forsaken by all. In the critical moment they had fled leaving Him alone to the tender mercies of wicked men, who had now cruelly scourged and beaten Him.

With quivering body and breaking heart the Son of Man was silent; for the cold kiss of Judas was still upon His lips, and that bitterest of all sorrows the faithlessness and treachery of *friends* had just entered like a sharp iron into His loving and sensitive soul.

This silence of Jesus tells of His tender

humanity; and be it always remembered that the humanity of Christ is an everlasting, continuous, unchanging fact. What He was, He *is*. As much to-day as ever the same warm, throbbing human heart. Now, as ever, He is thrilled with our joys, and *feels* all our sorrows for " He *is* touched with the feeling of our infirmities."

In the midst of our teeming, toiling and pain-stricken multitudes, there still moves a holy Presence whose very garment is charged with healing and sympathy. In the still room where our loved one lies cold in death, there yet stands a gracious Form who puts the mourners out and whispers of life and hope. Now, as of yore, the graves of our gentle dead are bedewed with the Redeemer's tears. O men and women here is our imperishable consolation He ever lives, He ever loves, He ever *feels*.

In the light of these thoughts let us see what lessons may be learnt from the memorable

CHRIST'S THORN-CROWN.

tragedy in Pilate's hall. Are we also in that hall; and have we any share in the scarlet robe, the mock sceptre, the "all hail" of the soldiers and their cruel crown of thorns?

Now, there were four distinct classes or sections of the people implicated in the Redeemer's mock trial, condemnation, and crucifixion; these were the Disciples who *forsook* Him, the Jews who *rejected* Him, Pilate who *slighted* Him, and the Soldiers who *mocked* Him.

And to forsake, reject, slight or mock the Saviour is to be guilty of grieving Him anew, and crowning Him afresh with thorns.

Therefore the first lesson taught us is that—

THEY CROWN CHRIST WITH THORNS, WHO FORSAKE HIM IN HIS TRIAL HOUR.

The scene in Gethsemane is itself sufficient to teach us that there were wounds in that tender

CHRIST'S THORN-CROWN.

heart deeper and more painful than any crown of thorns. When most in need of sympathy, when His soul was "exceeding sorrowful even unto death," when well-nigh sinking beneath that awful agony He had begged His three beloved disciples, with pathos so deep and human as to be almost bordering on fear, to watch one hour with Him, they had signally and completely failed. Do you not feel the pained surprise in the words—" What, could ye not watch with Me one hour?" Again, "Watch and pray lest ye *enter* into temptation." Instead of watching they slept, and as they slept the betrayer drew near. Already, though they knew it not, they had entered into temptation: already they were within the outermost circles of that silent whirlpool whose strong, subtle current was rapidly drawing them into its terrible vortex.

For the soul that slumbers when she ought to watch, sleeps on the brink of danger and death. The spirit was overborne by the weariness of the

CHRIST'S THORN-CROWN.

flesh, and from this sleep they awoke to see close upon them in the light of gleaming torches a wild, excited crowd with loud, confusing voices and the tramp of hurrying feet. For a moment only they paused—then, outnumbered and terrified, in the darkness they fled.

Let us remember this—*the disciples ran away and the soldiers found the thorns*.

It is so to-day. When Christ's own forsake Him, the world plaits afresh its cruel thorn-crown. When disciples fall away, "they crucify to themselves the Son of God afresh and put Him to an open shame." Mark how the lip of supercilious scorn curls at the notorious defection of a professing Christian. Hear the mocking jibe and jeer when a good man has fallen. "These are your Religious people!" It is the tragedy of the Redeemer's trial over again; the disciples have fled and the world is plaiting the crown of thorns; Christ is left alone

CHRIST'S THORN-CROWN.

and His enemies are mocking and smiting Him.

Now we know, from our Lord's sublime prayer on the Cross, that the mock homage and rude insolence of the soldiers moved only to pity the great sad heart of Jesus. Theirs was the sin of ignorance and He graciously forgave. Moreover their hypocrisy was, to use a paradox, sincere. They meant to mock and their meaning was not concealed. They were scorners, and openly avowed their scorn with jibe and jeer and blow. That deepest of wounds *a friend's treachery* they could not inflict. Their thorns tore His flesh, but did not wound His spirit like the faithlessness of His friends : for as there is no joy like the joy of a friend, so there are no wounds like those "wherewith I was wounded in the house of my *friends*."

The spiritual dulness of Philip, the kiss of Judas, the denial of Peter, the doubt of Thomas, make wounds far deeper than the thorns in His

CHRIST'S THORN-CROWN.

pale brow, or the nails in His quivering frame.

He feels more keenly than words can tell the drowsiness of His nearest followers, the cold kiss of nightly betrayal, the cowardly flight in the hour of trial, the following afar off in the darkness, the guilty silence broken by the base and passionate denial. Lips that once have moved under the resistless spell of Transfiguration bliss, wound more deeply than two-edged swords when they are frozen in craven dumbness, or when they of all lips are heard vehemently declaring—" I know not the man."

O you who have been with Christ when His garment has shone with unearthly glory, you who in moments of holy ecstasy have caught glimpses and visions of the Eternal Loveliness, or kneeling with Him in the starless Gethsemane of life's keenest agonies and profoundest mysteries, have there beheld the angel's face, and felt his touch, do not you above all others forsake Him and flee,

CHRIST'S THORN-CROWN.

for your faithlessness would pierce His very heart. Remember the question put to the apostate disciple—" Did not I see thee in the garden with Him?" Remember that *you have been identified with Christ,* and that if you draw back or fall away His name will be covered with shame, His brow crowned afresh with thorns.

If, like Judas and the disciples, we "know the place" of prayer (John 18 c. 2 v.) let us take care that we do not make it the place of slumber, betrayal or flight.

But this thrilling narrative also teaches us that:—

THEY CROWN CHRIST WITH THORNS WHO REJECT HIM AS THEIR SAVIOUR.

And this was the attitude of the Jews: they did not slight or ignore the kingly pretensions and royal claims of Jesus—they rejected them with violent scorn. The inscription of the

CHRIST'S THORN-CROWN.

Roman Governor, written at the dictation of his uneasy conscience, brought upon him the scornful protest of wounded pride—" Write not the King of the Jews, but that *he said* I am King of the Jews."

Who then were the real persecutors of Jesus? Who were really responsible for the scourging, the crown of thorns, the shameful death? The answer is clear—" His blood be upon us, and upon our children." He fell a victim not to the hatred of the openly profligate and profane, for that was the noblest of eulogies though ironically spoken, " Friend of publicans and sinners."

Thieves, murderers, and harlots felt the magnetic spell of His wondrous sympathy; and the common people oppressed with suffering, want, and care were irresistibly drawn to Him.

Ah, no—it was those sanctimonious religionists who deemed it a heinous sin to eat with "unwashen hands," the very men whom Christ had denounced as "whited sepulchres," who did not scruple to hound on Pilate and the people to destroy Him. Men who mistook ritual for piety, and hand-washing for heart-purity; who punctiliously observed the ceremonial law, but broke the law of *love:* men whose religion was a something put on *ab extra*, like a garment; not an inward, warm, spontaneous life of loving self-surrender.

It is a most suggestive and ominous fact that *it was the Church, and not the world, which rejected and crucified Christ.* The chief priests, scribes, and pharisees were, above all others, guilty of His blood : for the *instigator* is the true murderer.

Sirs, there is a terrible rejecting of Christ done in a religious way : there is such a thing as crowning the Lord with thorns under the

CHRIST'S THORN-CROWN.

inspiration of religious zeal.—" Saul, Saul, why persecutest thou Me?"

I may be very religious, yet far from God.

This truth is taught with great force and clearness in the fine contrast between the pharisee and publican. The former was a punctilious observer of ceremonial law; yet the real man emerges in the sanctimonious sneer at "this publican." A religious, but not a good man. The publican brings no offering but a broken heart, and is nearer God. If our religion allow us to remain, like the religionists of Christ's day, hard, over-reaching, proud, worldly, intolerant; if it do not chasten, ennoble, and sweeten our life, then it is only a solemn mockery and sorrowful delusion; we offer the Redeemer a crown— but of thorns!

Again we may learn from the conduct of Pilate that:—

CHRIST'S THORN-CROWN.

THEY CROWN CHRIST WITH THORNS WHO ARE GUILTY OF SLIGHTING HIM.

For the attitude of Pilate towards Jesus was far from the bitter hatred and jealous hostility of the Jews. The action of the Roman Governor in tampering with his conscience to appease the clamorous crowd, and above all to avoid the possible censure of Cæsar should he "let this man go," was miserably wrong; yet it was the vacillation of a *weak* man, rather than the intentional wrong-doing of a wicked one. Pilate's mistake was indecision, born of selfish fear. Knowing the innocence of the accused One, yet rather than face adverse public opinion and lose the friendship of Cæsar, he violated conscience and gave up Christ.

The name of the man who does this is always Pilate. Pilate is the man who has many a struggle with conscience, but whose higher nature succumbs to the lower; who has no hostility towards Jesus, yet will do a crooked deed

CHRIST'S THORN-CROWN.

rather than sacrifice worldly gain, or risk social status. Position, influence, wealth, popularity are more to him than an undefiled conscience; and "Society" is more than Christ.

Now, in such a man there may be no enmity towards God but, rather, too strong an attachment to the world. The real crown is given to Mammon, the mock crown to Jesus.

For at my bar, no less than at Pilate's, the patient Nazarene waits for judgment; and the solemn enquiry which stirred the troubled conscience of the Roman Governor I too must put to my own heart—" What shall I do then with Jesus which is called Christ?" I cannot escape this question. No washing of the hands can clear my soul if I slight Him. True, the historic incident has passed, but the spiritual tragedy proceeds. And still He sits assailed by the cruel mockeries of men, still the scarlet robe is upon Him, still the reed is in His hand, still

CHRIST'S THORN-CROWN.

the crown of thorns is tearing His brow, still they are leading Him away to Calvary. Perhaps I too have no enmity towards Christ; yet if, like Pilate, my real God is the world, then I am not guiltless of that crown of thorns.

Lastly we may learn that :—

THEY CROWN CHRIST WITH THORNS WHO OFFER HIM FALSE HOMAGE.

Let this solemn thought search your heart like a sunbeam. Is my professed adhesion to the Lord merely formal and nominal? Am I crying "Hail King" with my lips, while true devotion is absent from my heart? Then, I too am amongst the soldiers, for I partake of their spirit. Outwardly they worshipped, they cried " Hail King," they bowed the knee: but inwardly their minds were darkened, their hearts frivolous and insincere. Is my spirit in the least degree like theirs? Am I also hypocritical, insincere, frivolous, hard? If so, am not I too pressing the

CHRIST'S THORN-CROWN.

thorns into His bleeding brow? For consider what a confession of Christ's Kingship really implies, and bear in mind what true worship really is. It is yielding to the Lord heart, will, intellect, possessions, ALL—until the full current of our being set towards Him as the river to the boundless sea. It is to yearn with all the soul to know, to do, and to love His will. It is to be so penetrated and quickened by Christ's in-dwelling as that every *thought* shall be brought into subjection to His holy love and law.

Self-giving, self-consecration, self-offering is the only true and acceptable worship. Nothing is easier than to offer the Redeemer lip-worship, to cry "all hail," and to bow the knee: but He yearns for *soul-worship,* the offering of the life to Him. "Why call ye me Lord, Lord, and do not the things that I say?"—there is the grief, there the Crown of Thorns, there the Cross.

Our insincerity, indifference, inconsistency,

CHRIST'S THORN-CROWN.

disobedience, hypocrisy, these are the Saviour's thorn-crown; and he misunderstands this tragedy altogether who cannot read between the lines, and who does not see that both Pilate's hall and Calvary are in his own heart.

Yet why should not the past suffice for the grief and pain we have given the Redeemer? The past is gone, irreparable, dead; no longer ours. Let us forget it. Grieving over yesterday only serves to sap the energies of to-day.

Look not back.

Behind us are Gethsemane's heavy slumbers and dark flight, the denial and the crown of thorns: before us is the future, an opening dawn, fresh and bright with unknown possibilities.

Of the guilty past the Saviour speaks not a word. See; His eyes, filled with the strange, sweet light of the morning, are searching thee

CHRIST'S THORN-CROWN.

through and through, as He tenderly asks :— "Lovest thou Me?" Sorrowful memories crowd upon thee as the response of chastened, loving penitence trembles on the lip :—" Lord Thou knowest all things, Thou knowest that I love Thee."

In the past I have crowned Thee with thorns, but henceforth will I crown Thee with LOVE.

THE KINGDOM AND THE KEYS.

"I will give unto thee the Keys of the Kingdom of Heaven." S. MATTHEW 16 C., 19 V.

IT has often happened that in the heat, bitterness and confusion of theological debate, some solemn and beautiful truth, in the very words under discussion, has been utterly lost sight of; so that instead of discovering those rich veins of gold which are there, men have done little but raise heaps of contention to cover them.

Thus, by sorrowful ingenuity, we have sometimes turned light into darkness, and extracted only poison from sweetest flowers.

Such for example has, in some measure, been

THE KINGDOM AND THE KEYS.

the fate of our Lord's singularly striking words to S. Peter—" I will give unto thee the keys of the kingdom of Heaven." But whatever may have been their peculiar significance as applied to S. Peter, all thoughtful minds will at once feel their great beauty and force as regards every living soul: for in a very real sense these memorable words belong to every human being.

There is not a man in the whole world who does not hold the keys: for the keys symbolize these two great principles—*Authority* and *Responsibility*—influence over one's fellowmen, and accountability to God for the right use of our trust.

Whoever has power to sway the minds of men; whoever possesses influence, however small, over human hearts; whoever has talents, many or few; stands in the great house of life at once a master and a servant, a lord and a steward—for life's lordship and its stewardship are but two

THE KINGDOM AND THE KEYS.

sides of the same truth. We may only have " a few things " entrusted to us, but to be faithful over these, to rule well the small kingdom now given to our care, is to prove our fitness for greater kingdoms hereafter—" I will make thee ruler over many."

So the kingdom, spoken of in our text we, are ruling *now;* and the keys are those talents, gifts, and graces with which we may open men's hearts and minds, thus letting Light, Love, Beauty—*Christ* into the soul.

.   .   .

Let me therefore speak first of the Kingdom of Heaven, what it is, and what it is to be in it; and secondly, permit me to show how we may open the Kingdom to others, and to point out particularly some keys we may use in this glorious endeavour to save men from sin, and death; leading them out of darkness into " His marvellous light."

THE KINGDOM AND THE KEYS.

THE KINGDOM OF HEAVEN.

How repeatedly these words—"the Kingdom of Heaven" fell from the lips of Jesus! This beautiful, tuneful phrase runs through the whole of His ministry like the refrain of some sweet, familiar hymn. Hence, if we would understand our Lord and His teaching, it is essential to gain the clearest idea as to the meaning of this constantly recurring phrase.

What then is a Kingdom? It is the domain of a King—the territory and people under his sceptre. In this sense it indicates the reign of a person. Or the term may be used impersonally as pointing to the reign of a principle, as when we speak of the animal or vegetable or mineral kingdom. When "the Kingdom of God" is the expression employed the prominent idea is the reign of a Person—the King of Kings and Lord of Lords; but when the alternate phrase "the Kingdom of Heaven" is used, stress is laid on the principle of heavenly-mindedness—purity of

THE KINGDOM AND THE KEYS.

heart which reigns and rules in those who belong to this Kingdom.

Now, there should be no haze over our minds regarding this heavenly Kingdom; for it always lay before the eye of Christ like some green, lovely land all blossoming in beauty, a sunlit, enchanted place—before Him yet always with Him—a glorious May-morning about Him everywhere.

And for this, and this above all else, He lived that life of love and tears, and died upon the Cross,—that He might bring all sorts and conditions of people, tired old age, strenuous manhood, hopeful youth, happy childhood, into this Kingdom.

O brethren this was, this *is* the sublime passion of Jesus to save men from sin, suffering, death: to bring them out of the realms of Night and Despair into the glad morning of a new and

THE KINGDOM AND THE KEYS.

better Life — to save them for righteousness, holiness, peace, heaven—God : this was the holy dream that haunted Him by day and by night, and that drew Him to the hills to spend whole nights in prayer after He had exhausted Himself in whole days of toil. This *is* His dream still— the ineffable Vision—the universal reign of the King of Heaven—*the Summer shining there, far beyond the last Winter that shall ever be.* "For He must reign till He hath put all enemies under His feet."

Then will be the final triumph of the Kingdom; meanwhile let us remember that multitudes are already under its gracious sway : for the Kingdom is not a Somewhere, not a fair Country whose verdant hills and flashing rivers lie far above the fleecy clouds, away up in the sky—not a royal City with jasper walls, gates of pearl and crystal, gorgeous palaces, glittering towers, and streets of gold. It is not a "new Jerusalem" in Heaven above, but a City "coming down from

THE KINGDOM AND THE KEYS.

God out of Heaven :"—Yes *coming down!* For "the tabernacle of God is with men"—not with angels and redeemed spirits only—but with men, and "He will dwell with them."

Hence our Lord proclaimed the Kingdom "at hand" and again "within you," while S. Paul declares the divine Love to be "shed abroad in the heart :" *shed abroad*—like the dawn blushing over land and sea.

Now, the Kingdom knows no local, geographical, boundary lines, for it is the Kingdom of LOVE—and love is measureless : or to transpose the figure, Love is the Angel which alone can measure this new Jerusalem. It is a City whose gates stand open on the East, West, North, and South ; and wherever love is, there is the Kingdom.

> "The mind is its own place
> And in itself can make
> A heaven of hell, a hell of heaven."

THE KINGDOM AND THE KEYS.

But although this divine Kingdom be all around us, like a May-morning, yet we may be far from it; as light, pouring on the sightless eyeballs of the blind child, leaves him in darkness still. See Christ yonder, in the midst of the throng who press upon Him, but understand Him not—for "the Light shineth in darkness and the darkness comprehendeth it not,"—till one soul *sees* and one withered hand with eager, nervous, trembling finger is stretched out to touch His garment.—It is enough—the deed is done—and the light of sweet health and peace is flooding one sad life now sad no more. For there is a touch that heals and saves.

To know that Christ is near yet not to *touch* Him, to feel that the Kingdom is "at hand" yet to keep outside it; to be conscious that we are bathed in the light and love of God, yet to keep our eyes and hearts fast closed against it all—alas this is the pitiful tragedy of many a human heart.

THE KINGDOM AND THE KEYS.

The lost thief perished within reach of Christ, without a sigh of appeal to Him whose dear heart was breaking for the love He bore the lost.

But there *is* a touch that opens that wondrous heart of Love, and fills our own with heaven—"To-day thou shalt be with me in Paradise!" O what an opening of the Kingdom, what a flinging wide of the pearly gates, what a breaking of day over the dark inner world of that confused and wasted life!

See how the Sun shines on all the glad earth to-day; but yonder little flower is stubbornly closing its petals and turning day into night. Foolish flower perishing in darkness though bathed in light. Touch the flower, throw back its closed petals, open its heart to the Sun, bring it forth into bright, warm summer.

Poor perishing man who will not come to

THE KINGDOM AND THE KEYS.

Christ that he might have Life, dying in darkness though baptized in Light. Go, touch his heart; open it—for you can—bring him forth into the Kingdom of Light, Heaven, God.

Wordsworth exquisitely says " Heaven lies about us in our infancy," yet that is only the heaven of innocence. About the pure in heart lies the sweeter heaven of divine Peace: for virtue is more than innocence, and it is "to him that *overcometh* will I grant to sit with Me in My Throne." The Kingdom and the Throne are not the rewards of innocence that is ignorant of sin because it has not yet felt its subtle charm, but they are the priceless recompense of the virtue that, at whatever cost, repels and conquers sin. This is that violence which our Lord tells us is able to take the Kingdom by force—the plucking out of the eye, the severing of hand or foot—alas that gates so strait and ways so narrow should lie between us and LIFE.

. . . . . .

THE KINGDOM AND THE KEYS.

If then it be true that light is all around, yet men are perishing in darkness, what can you and I do to save the dying? Why, we can open hearts and open the Kingdom of Heaven if only we will use the Keys the Master has placed in our hands.

Let us now turn our thoughts to—

THE KEYS.

As already said the keys indicate the steward, while they point to his authority on the one hand, and to his responsibility and accountability to his Lord on the other.

Sirs, we are all stewards in the great house of life, and in our hands are the keys of power and influence over our fellowmen. Such keys are our talents, gifts, graces, and opportunities which we may use either to open, or to close, the Kingdom of Heaven to human souls every day

THE KINGDOM AND THE KEYS.

—for in a very real and solemn sense it is true that every man is his brother's keeper.

To let talent lie idle or to waste it ; to put one's personal influence to ignoble or wicked uses ; to squander and fritter away our life ; to prostitute our gifts, whether great or small, to evil ends—all this is to shut the Kingdom of Heaven in the face of our dying brother.

But use our gifts aright ; let our personal influence be on the side of Christ as against sin, and we are opening the Kingdom before our brother whether he himself shall, or shall not, enter in and be saved.

And now to give the message clearness and point let me remind you of some of the keys entrusted to our hands.

For example there is—

THE KINGDOM AND THE KEYS.

THE KEY OF SOME SPECIAL TALENT.

Think for instance what a key the musical composer holds in his keeping,—the maker and blender of harmonies! What subtle faculty is his to fascinate the ear, fire the imagination, soothe or thrill the soul, bearing it up on soaring wings to realms unseen, infinite, eternal; and very literally opening kingdoms of bliss.

Or the poet with his seraph spirit and that eye of his "with a fine frenzy rolling," how he opens our dull ears to the melodies of Nature, and quickens our dim eyes to catch the beatific Vision! Every star and flower aflame with glory; every bush, like that at Horeb, a tongue of fire. Even the stones of the valley are a ladder reaching to the Throne and bring us dreams of Angels and of Heaven. Or the sound of many waters is the voice of the Lord, and the rainbow is seen about the Throne.

Mark too the orator, whose superb gifts of

THE KINGDOM AND THE KEYS.

speech and suasion play upon an audience as upon an instrument of many strings ; see how the laughter comes in sudden flashes, like bursts of sunshine across the landscape on a cloudy day ; and now watch the deepening attention, the solemn feeling showing in a thousand faces, the tears gathering and falling like passing showers. The ancients represented the orator with chains of gold coming from his lips, to indicate that he could draw men with his eloquence at his own sweet will. They might have painted him with keys of gold in his hand, for to him it is given to open kingdoms of glory. An orator once advertized that he would heal diseases with words !

Or again, see the teacher at work, and mark what a magical key is the gift of imparting knowledge. As the word implies, the true educator is a leader out, for he leads out the pupil's mind to new lands, unknown realms, and as yet unconquered kingdoms. How subtle

THE KINGDOM AND THE KEYS.

and deft is his art. He finds the springs of thought and feeling; inspires confidence and wins affection; trains the learner's intellect; calls forth his latent powers; reveals the pupil to himself, and opens out sunlit lands before him. This was the key Philip used when he opened the Kingdom of Heaven to the eunuch.

In a word, all special gifts are, very really, keys for opening kingdoms. The artist who can suggest infinity on a square inch of canvas; the hymn-writer who lifts the soul to the gates of heaven; the author who knows the secret of the human heart, and can stir its noblest passions till feeling resolves itself into deeds of love; the architect who moulds granite into myriad forms of beauty, drawing music out of stones; the sculptor at whose magic touch the marble wastes, but the angel grows. These are but some illustrations of the keys, and of their varied uses in the countless walks of life.

THE KINGDOM AND THE KEYS.

Still further. Though you possess no special talent, yet in your hand also are the keys. *Every living soul is a centre of moral influence, and to be good is more than to be great.* For as the tiniest atom, floating in the sunbeam, affects the Earth's centre of gravity, and helps to guide her in her path through space; so the least significant amongst us is helping to direct, for good or ill, the destiny of the race.

Hence there is—

THE KEY OF PERSONAL INFLUENCE.

And who can doubt the almost irresistible charm of a truly Christ-like life? In such a life Heaven lies mirrored as the sky in the lake. Would you know what the Kingdom of Heaven is—see there, it shines in yonder man.

" *Ye* are our Epistles read and known of all men."

THE KINGDOM AND THE KEYS.

Men do not read the Bible: it is literally a dead-letter-thing to the vast majority; but they read Christ's living, incarnate letters; and, through them, find their way to the Kingdom.

"Do you believe in the love of God?"—said a gentlewoman to a poor unfortunate in a hospital ward. "I did not," whispered the dying girl, "I did not *till I knew you*, but you have made me believe in it." The Kingdom stood open for her in the face of that true sister of mercy.

The truth is, most men do not believe in printed creeds: they believe or disbelieve in *men*.

The author of "Tom Brown's School Days" knew this; he knew that it is through the human we reach the Divine. Hence he has let the curtain fall with Tom standing at his old master's tomb at Rugby, the tears filling his manly eyes as the thought, like a sudden revelation, flashes

THE KINGDOM AND THE KEYS.

through him, that it was through this man, now cold in death, he had first learnt to love Christ. It was Christ in Arnold the boy had loved, though not in those days had he understood this.

Let us live so that those who know us will think of Christ when their thoughts touch us. It was once said " They have been with Jesus."

Again—it is hardly necessary to do more than name—

THE GOLDEN KEY OF WEALTH.

It can open kingdoms : it can unlock many doors. If you possess this key, do not forget the great responsibility such a trust involves ; or the untold joy its right use brings. Never was Heaven nearer to you than when you found that soul in sadness, crushed to the ground, a tender plant borne down by the storm. Hope had almost fled, light had nearly gone, the spirit was nigh broken. Your heart was touched.

THE KINGDOM AND THE KEYS.

You went yourself to the sufferer, you poured in oil and wine, lent your beast, opened your purse. It was not so much in the gift itself that the loveliness of the deed lay, but in the dear human sympathy that prompted you.

Be rich in good works, "ready to distribute," for so shall you open kingdoms of joy to many. To few indeed is this key entrusted, but they who use it well are amongst Christ's truest friends. "The poor ye have always with you," and "inasmuch as ye have done it unto one of the least of these, my brethren, ye have done it unto ME."

Nor must we forget—

THE KEY OF PRAYER.

Do you remember that, upon one occasion, when our Lord ceased praying, the disciples said "Lord, teach us to pray." The rich music of that prayer had trembled into silence, and left them longing for more. While He prayed all

THE KINGDOM AND THE KEYS.

Heaven stood open. There are those with us to-day who possess, in no small degree, this strange power. So simple is their faith; so mighty their hold of God; so clear their vision of Eternal realities; so close their intimacy with Heaven; that to be near them when they pray, is to kneel on the threshold of Glory. So much more is in their prayer, than in the words they utter.

And as Elijah's prayer opened the sky, bringing down the gracious baptism of rain, and making the glad earth, as if born from above, spring into green, new life—so will our prayer open Heaven and bring down sweet Life and Love to men.

There is yet another key which is ever opening the kingdoms of joy; and, which, by its gentle touch, opens hearts that long have been fast closed. It is—

THE KINGDOM AND THE KEYS.

THE KEY OF BROTHERLY-LOVE.

In one of the sublimest passages ever penned, S. Paul sings to the praise of love. "Faith, Hope, Charity, these three, but the greatest of these is Charity." The Revised Version better translates this word—love—but there is no exact equivalent in English for the Greek word. "Charity" is much too cold, conventional, and prosaic to express the glow and pathos in the Apostle's mind and heart; while "love" has acquired an application too specific, and does not indicate, in ordinary speech, that deep, wide, reverential feeling of love and devotion to all men, which explains the consuming zeal of the Apostles, and the divine self-sacrifice of our dear Redeemer.

It is *spiritual, heavenly love,* as distinguished from mere personal affection or friendship—precious though they be. It is to love our fellowmen as Christ loved them, for the grand possibilities of immortal life and infinite beauty wrapt up in them. To love a dying thief not for what he was, or had been, but because of what he would become; as the mother sees in the puling babe the glorious man that is to be, and reinforces her love with thoughts of the future—a well-spring of perennial HOPE.

To love men not merely for the sake of their secular and temporal welfare, but for their spiritual and eternal well-being too, this is to love with the Redeemer's passion. And such love, full of tender human sympathy, goes about doing good in ten thousand quiet, unobtrusive ways.

Key—did we call it? The figure will do—but one ought rather to call this grace the Angel in the soul, the heaven of love within. "He that dwelleth in love, dwelleth in God, and God in him:" for, "God is love."

The little shell, on the sea-shore, cannot contain the great ocean; yet all the essence of

THE KINGDOM AND THE KEYS.

the sea may be in its tiny cavity. Even so the divine Love may dwell in the human heart.

It is related that on a hot summer-day there lay in a gutter, just outside a city, a young man about twenty-five years of age. He lay helpless and unconscious, in the stupor of intoxication. People came that way, but either did not observe him, or "passed by on the other side." By and bye, a poor woman in black came quietly near. She looked upon the young fellow with the hot sun scorching his brain. Her woman's heart stood still. What could she do? He was too heavy for her to lift, too far gone to be reasoned with. She took out her handkerchief, spread it over his face and forehead to screen him from the sun, and walked away. Presently he awoke from his stupor, removed the handkerchief from his face, and conscience spoke. "I have sunk very low, God knows," he said, " but somebody has pitied me; and if I am not too low to be pitied, I am not too low to be

THE KINGDOM AND THE KEYS.

saved." That woman in black we may think of now as an angel in white; for when by her simple, loving act, and thoughtful, tender pity, she touched the heart and roused the conscience of this man, she was opening the Kingdom of Heaven to untold throngs of human souls: for that man became one of the greatest temperance orators the world has ever known; and countless families owe to John B. Gough their rescue from sin, misery, and death.

O Brothers, the Kingdom of Heaven, the Kingdom of Light and Love is AT HAND and just outside, "not far from the Kingdom," are men, women, and little children whom we may save. And to spur us to fresh effort in this holy toil—listen—for the highest of all Voices is speaking to every one of us:—"I will give unto thee the Keys of the Kingdom of Heaven."

THE KINGDOM AND THE KEYS.

THE KEYS OF THE KINGDOM.
The night is dark and dreary,
   So cold and damp and sad,
No light to cheer the weary,
   No fire to make them glad.
Have you the key to strengthen
   The famished one from death,
Relieve and gently soften
   The last and hard-drawn breath?

Or in the marble mansion
   Where wealth and gold abound,
What saddened hearts are broken,
   For naught of love is found!
Have you the key to reach them
   To soothe them in their grief,
Some sympathy and pity
   To render sweet relief?

THE KINGDOM AND THE KEYS.

But see that weak soul wandering
   Blind-groping, ne'er a spark
Of light to lead him over
   The dread expanse of dark.
Have you the keys to open
   The portals curtained tight,
And raise from night to morning
   This soul to worlds of light?

Then hesitate no longer,
   But give the needy rest,
Sore hearts are tired and yearning
   For peace upon His breast.
The keys of His bright Kingdom
   Are lying in *your* hand,
Oh haste unlock the secret
   Of Life within that Land.

H. M. C.

GETHSEMANE.

(A WORD TO THE SORROWFUL.)

"A place called Gethsemane."

S. MATTHEW 26 C., 36 V.

LET us go to Gethsemane. Let us approach that sacred garden with silent and reverent steps, and look with trembling on that memorable scene; a scene whose sublimity we may *feel*, but cannot comprehend.

Amidst that "darkness visible" dwells the everlasting light—a mystery—a revelation—a bitter pain—a deep, unutterable joy.

It was Passover that night, and through the

GETHSEMANE.

open gate of the city, our Lord and His disciples —all, save one, the betrayer—had passed into the road leading to Bethany, and there, half a mile from the city walls the little group paused, while Jesus went with His three favourite followers, beneath the spreading branches of the olive trees, into the quiet darkness. Only the stars peeped, here and there, between the broad leaves, as if their spiritual rays should say—" though Earth may not behold, all Heaven is watching."

Why did the Master confer so high a privilege on those three, Peter, James, and John, as to allow them to be near that hallowed spot? What need had the Son of God for their presence in that trying hour? Was it not that He was also Son of *Man*, and felt the need of human sympathy? He could better bear the coming agony if those who loved Him were near at hand. But they *slept!* Alas, how often do we also sleep, unconscious that close by are souls struggling in the agonies of sorrow, temptation, or

GETHSEMANE.

death. The world is a great Gethsemane where three sleep while one agonizes and prays.

And mark, even the privileged three could not follow Jesus to the wrestling spot, for He bade them "stay here" while He withdrew a little distance to pray. *Christ, felt, as we do, the limits of human sympathy.* When our loved ones have done their utmost, the wine-press must be trodden alone. So long as the sorrow does not completely overwhelm, their presence comforts and strengthens; but there is a stage beyond this, a deep, awful feeling of loneliness which man's sympathy is impotent to meet. At such times, there is in the central deeps of our being, a fathomless void into which human voices call in vain, for they awake no echo. Such a moment was this in the Redeemer's life. Those who have felt it all, know how the soul yearns, in that hour, to be alone.

And what is this yearning for solitude? It

GETHSEMANE.

is the cry of the spirit after God: it is not a desire to escape sympathy, but a craving for the holiest, the divinest, the only perfect sympathy. "Alone," said the Saviour,—"yet not alone, for the Father is with me."

Ah grief-stricken soul, driven by sorrow into that lonely place, know you not that in the solitude is GOD? The wind, the earthquake, and the fire have swept by—and now in the "still, small voice" that breaks the desert-silence, the Lord is drawing near.

Now we observe that—

GETHSEMANE WAS A PLACE OF HEART-RENDING CONFLICT.

Do not, for a moment, imagine that the conflict was between evil and good, sin and holiness, hell and Heaven. A thousand times NO! It was a struggle between the human and the Divine. For although Christ was human,

GETHSEMANE.

He was without sin; and that is only a human, not a sinful cry—" Father, if it be possible, let this cup pass from me." Reproach not yourself, poor sufferer, if under crushing sorrow and in view of bitter trial, this cry should also wring your heart. Jesus uttered it; and it will ever abide the sinless and natural cry of the sorrowful and broken spirit.

True, indeed, it is not for us to fathom the sacred mystery of Christ's grief; nor can our dim eyes penetrate the shades of His Gethsemane. There is a point beyond which we, like Peter, James, and John, may not go. But we know that while His one yearning desire was to do the Father's Will, yet He agonized in prayer to be spared the cup. And with us, at least, this is the real test, this the fearful struggle, when we are wedded to our own wills, yet feel that they are crossing and challenging the Will of God. Still more severe is the conflict when there is no consciousness of sin in the desires and feelings

GETHSEMANE.

we cannot repress; nay, when they themselves are the very gift of Heaven.

It is when some love, lawful, pure, and beautiful in itself, is brought face to face with love to the Father—as when the pale Mother watches, with bleeding heart, her dying child, and inwardly cries " let this cup pass from me "—ah, it is then, when a love sweet and holy, a love itself inbreathed by God, chafes and murmurs at that yet higher and holier Love—this is the heart-rending—this is our Gethsemane. For the sorest trial is never in the struggle between evil and good; never in the denial of our baser self to follow the higher, because here duty is always plain, and the voice of Conscience clear. Gethsemane, on the other hand, is the conflict within the soul, of two *pure* loves.

But what was it that made the Son of God to tremble and agonize? Can it be possible that He who alone was serenely calm amidst the

GETHSEMANE.

roaring billows of the Galilean lake, and who chided hardy fishermen for their timidity and lack of faith, was now unmanned in the prospect of death? What fear could Christ have of death? Had He not killed death and set its prisoners free? Had not His voice charmed the dead back to life, as the voice of Spring recalls the flowers?

Ah, it was something deadlier than death that awed and almost paralyzed that loving heart! The serpent's fang was piercing Him. Deadly hatred for yearning love—was not this Christ's cross? Sin leading the world captive, and crucifying the Love of God. Now the Redeemer's perfect sympathy with men made Him feel all this as though He were Himself guilty. " He bore our sins;" and, amongst these sins, the *shame* of the Cross which men did not feel. As a good son feels the sin and shame of his rebellious brother, and will interpose himself to save him from the just recompense of his guilt.

GETHSEMANE.

Love suffers with the loved-one, and suffers *for* him.

Add to this the foreshadowing of that awful darkness which not only hid the Father's face, but almost destroyed the consciousness of His all-enfolding Presence; and do you wonder at Christ's agony and bloody sweat? Do you wonder that Gethsemane was a place of heart-rending conflict?

Further, you will observe that because of this conflict—

GETHSEMANE WAS A PLACE OF SORROWFUL DARKNESS.

For as two rays of light, meeting, produce darkness; so it would seem that the Redeemer's natural desire to escape the bitter cup, and on the other hand His longing to do the Father's Will, created for the moment, a fierce struggle in His breast. And truly it was as if the gloom of that

GETHSEMANE.

night had crept into His heart, and thrown its mantle of thick shadows round His soul. For a brief moment, only, the night seemed starless, and Christ's pure spirit grew dark and sorrowful beneath the overhanging storm. The ocean, which but lately mirrored the glittering stars, is now darkened by the gathering clouds, and troubled by the rising winds.

Sensitive hearts tremble in the prospect of trial ; not from fear, but from the intensity of their affections. For it belongs to sensitive natures to feel life's joys and sorrows with tenfold degree ; as the tears of Jesus were, at once, the reward and the penalty of His divine tenderness.

And always, to the bravest, the anticipation of trouble is harder to bear than the trial itself, as the hour before the battle tests the most courageous soldier. We can bear anything better than *suspense;* for this is terrible. A

GETHSEMANE.

vague unrest disturbs the spirit, and fills us with indescribable awe. The coming trouble rises before the mind vast, fearful, swollen, and exaggerated, through the medium of our fears, as hills loom into mountains through the haze of twilight. The cup is bitterest not when it is at the lips; but when the will cannot, as yet, bend to the trial. There is a sense in which Gethsemane is darker than Calvary.

But see, while now the night is darkest—see through the rifted clouds that shining star! Hark!

"My Father."

O thrice blessed ray of holy light. The problem is solved now; the grief is bearable; the shadows are fleeing away. The soul that has not lost the sense of the Divine Fatherhood is far from despair, for despair can never cry— "*My Father.*" So long as the heart can cry, "My Father," no sorrow, however heavy, can

GETHSEMANE.

break it; no trial, however keen, can make shipwreck of faith.

There is, indeed, a stoical spirit which possesses stern and unfeeling natures enabling them to meet trouble with stony indifference; but what a chasm parts this soul-less acquiescence in fate from the faith that gives up its dearest treasure, only saying, with quivering lip,—" My Father!" Fatalism is not Faith; Stoicism is not Christianity.

Further we note that—

GETHSEMANE WAS A SOLITARY PLACE.

Every place of trial is a *lonely* place. It is this loneliness which constitutes at once the severity and sublimity of sorrow. There is something peculiar in every heart making its own bitterness an unspeakable secret, and debarring the stranger from intermeddling with its joy. No one life is an exact copy of another. Every

GETHSEMANE.

man is unique. Every temptation is special and peculiar. Every follower of Jesus must bear his own cross. Every soul has her own Gethsemane, and must face its agony *alone*. And it is only then, when alone we have to bear the crushing grief, and alone encounter the bewildering trial, that we feel our utter helplessness, and realize how powerless is human sympathy to meet our deepest needs. In that hour when the desolating sorrow, like the hot simoon of the desert, parches all the flowers of life and withers its joy at a stroke, only the Father Himself can comfort and console. But there is a grandeur in this sacred solitude of grief which leaves its nobleness upon the stricken heart: there is a beauty in the chastened soul which belongs only to those who are the children of sorrow and "acquainted with grief." They passed, alone, into the shades of their Gethsemane; they have come back to us clothed with *the beauty of holiness*.

And into your Gethsemane none can go with

GETHSEMANE.

you. Even the nearest and dearest cannot follow to the wrestling spot. Peter, James, and John fall asleep. The wine-press must be trod alone.

But do not be alarmed if into some place of loneliness the Father has led you; for there are deep lessons which can only be learnt when the soul is thus brought face to face with the Eternal Love. The blind man must be led *out of the town,* before the Saviour can open his eyes. By wonderful ways the Father leads us to these lonely places, and in the solitude He touches the soul.

Like Jacob, in the dark night, we wrestle with the Unseen One, and the cry of our heart is—"tell me thy name," thou awful mystery! Why this struggle; why this broken peace; why this bleeding heart; why this bitter cup; why this fearful doubt, shuddering on the verge of despair? Is thy name cruel mockery or—— LOVE?

GETHSEMANE.

Enough that, in the wrestling, a new name has been given *us;* enough that our Gethsemane like Christ's, like Jacob's, has become our *Peniel*—the place where we, unclothed that we might be clothed upon, have seen God face to face.

Yet more—

GETHSEMANE WAS A PLACE OF TRIUMPH BECAUSE A PLACE OF SUBMISSION.

" Nevertheless, not as I will." He is far on in the Christ-life who can say, from the depths of his heart—" not as I will." How many—nay, how *few*, can truly say it! We imagine the lesson is learnt; we honestly believe that our wills are His, come what may; but when the storm breaks, and the bolt falls upon us, we are alarmed at the fearful vitality of self-will that frets and complains, if it does not *rebel*, because the Higher Will has challenged it.

Only Gethsemane teaches submission.

GETHSEMANE.

Then let us learn from this sublime Wrestler to bend our will to the Father's; let us strive to read into our own life these inspired words—"not as I will"—even though we do it with "agony and bloody sweat." Prosperity, fame, health, wealth, pleasure, popular applause, worldliness, can never teach this deep lesson; for it is one of those priceless possessions with which sorrow, and sorrow only, can enrich the soul.

How significant too the *name* of the garden, for Gethsemane means oil-press; and it was here the oil was squeezed out of the olives as they were crushed under the labourer's feet. Here also the soul of the Redeemer was crushed till the blood crimsoned His brow. Here the divinest of all teachings escaped His lips—"*Father, as Thou wilt.*"

And now the prostrate Wrestler is victorious; the human bows to the Divine; the higher Will triumphs; the spirit, not the flesh, is

GETHSEMANE.

enthroned, the heavenly, not the earthly, reigns.

> "Our wills are ours, we know not how;
> Our wills are ours, to make them *Thine.*"

He conquers self who bows to God.

Finally, let us never forget that

GETHSEMANE WAS A PLACE OF ANGELIC VISITATION.

S. Luke says — "and there appeared an angel unto Him, from Heaven, strengthening Him." In Gethsemane the Redeemer was strengthened for Calvary: the baptizm of suffering strengthened Him for Sacrifice.

It is even so with us. The trial once looked upon as a dark, dark visitant, becomes to the chastened and subdued spirit, a heavenly messenger. The thorn in the flesh, against which we prayed so earnestly, becomes a servant of

GETHSEMANE.

Heaven bringing to the soul grace upon grace that the power of Christ may rest on us. *Thus, every Gethsemane has its angel.*

Bow to the Divine Will, and in quiet submission, there will come to you a sweet calm—a peace, which, like the angel strengthening our Lord, will bring in its bosom new life, new hope, and new strength for further conflict.

Though it be impossible to take away the cup, the Father will send an angel to hold it to your lips, and *faith* will turn its bitterest dregs into the nectar of Heaven. If the thorn cannot be removed, yet He will give more abundant grace; and the conviction will grow within the breast that a gracious purpose underlies the suffering, and that the name of the mystery is—LOVE. You shall *feel* this, though you cannot fathom it—bright horizons far, far away, fresh as morning dew—all this shall be felt, as a blind child feels, but cannot see, the morning light.

GETHSEMANE.

But do not misunderstand. Gethsemane is still Gethsemane; pain is always pain; temptation is ever temptation; sorrow always sorrow. None can feel this so keenly as Christ did. Faith does not make pain to be no pain; but she changes it into a *purifier,* for trial always purifies him who bows to it as from God. And only him; for it is the contrite and humble heart alone which softens under pain. Fire melts gold, but it dries and hardens clay. Affliction is one thing to believing Job; it is quite another to his unbelieving wife. It only hardens the rebellious Pharoah; but it restores the erring and repentant David.

And it is *faith* alone; faith like Job's, like David's, like Christ's, which beholds—moving amidst the shades of Gethsemane, clothed in soft light—a heavenly Form; and feels, even in the darkest hour of sorrow
THE ANGEL'S TOUCH.

GETHSEMANE.

"GETHSEMANE."

In that dark Gethsemane
   Every sound was hushed,
Jesus entered wearily
   Heart and soul pain-crushed.

Oh the bitter suffering
   Of that silent hour,
When the Saviour agonized
   'Gainst the tempter's power.

'Lone, yet not alone was He
   Thro' that hard-fought fight,
For a cry rose from His lips
   Piercing thro' the night—

With the blood-sweat on His brow
   Hear that Voice divine!
"Father, let this cup pass by
   If *Thy* will—not mine."

GETHSEMANE.

Cruel struggle sharp and sad,
    Now forever done,
For the blessed Son of Man
    Victory has won.

Then an angel's radiant form
    Thro' the twilight dim,
Laden rich with love and joy,
    Comes to strengthen Him.

So when we deep-drowned in grief,
    Weeping, strive for Right,
There, in our Gethsemane
    Stands an Angel white!

                    H. M. C.

www.ingramcontent.com/pod-product-compliance
Lightning Source LLC
Chambersburg PA
CBHW020901230426
43666CB00008B/1269